PORTERS

ENGLISH

COOKERY BIBLE

Ancient and Modern

Richard, Earl of Bradford,
and Carol Wilson

**ROBSON
BOOKS**

To all the dedicated staff at Porters, who have worked hard to maintain its success over 25 years.

First published in the United Kingdom in 2005 by
Robson Books,
10 Southcombe Street
London
W14 0RA

An imprint of Anova Books Company Ltd

Reprinted 2007

ISBN 9781861057372

A catalogue record for this title is available from the British Library.

Designed by Richard Mason
Typeset by SX Composing DTP, Rayleigh, Essex
Printed and bound by MPG Books Ltd, Bodmin, Cornwall

This book can be ordered direct from the publisher.
Contact the marketing department, but try your bookshop first.

www.anovabooks.com

Notes on the Recipes

All recipes serve 4–6.
All spoon measures are level unless otherwise stated.
All eggs are medium.
Don't mix metric and imperial measures in one recipe – stick to one type.
If using a fan oven, check the manufacturer's directions. As a rule, reduce the oven temperature by 10–20°C (50-68°F). Cakes may take slightly less time to bake than stated in the recipe.
Unrefined sugars are used in the recipes. They retain the natural molasses present in sugar cane.

CONTENTS

✦

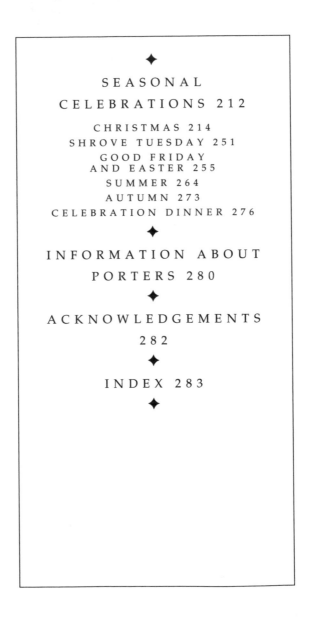

FOREWORD
BY RICHARD,
EARL OF BRADFORD

Once upon a time I had a dream to open a reasonably priced, real English restaurant in central London. Not aimed at the top end of the market, but somewhere with the fun atmosphere and friendly service of an American-style eatery, ensuring at the same time that it was family-friendly as well.

In 1978 I owned and helped run a delightful and thriving French restaurant, Bewicks, in Walton Street, London. But after two years of considerable success, including gaining a star in the prestigious *Egon Ronay Guide* in 1977 – 'Young, eager and enthusiastic management has transformed this Chelsea restaurant' – I knew that, with a mere 48 covers, it was too small to make serious money. Therefore I put my restaurant on the market and looked for a site to realise my English dream.

At that time the Covent Garden area was in a state of turmoil as the fruit and vegetable market where Eliza Doolittle sold her flowers in *My Fair Lady*, even though the film was actually all shot in a studio in Hollywood, had closed down and was being redeveloped. However, its location seemed brilliant to me – in the heart of Theatreland, with Fleet Street, in those days where most of the major newspapers had their offices, just down the road, well served by London Underground and buses and with plenty of businesses around – so I concentrated my search there.

When details came through for large premises in Henrietta Street, a mere 100 yards from the main market, with a glorious frontage of Victorian tiles and polished wood, it seemed more than perfect, it was absolutely ideal.

The natural English product to concentrate on, trying to compete with the Italian pizza or the American hamburger, was, in my view, the pie – capable of having a variety of fillings and toppings, of being prepared in bulk and easily served as an individual dish. The pies would naturally be accompanied by mashed potato, and the menu would also contain a wide choice of those wonderful British 'nursery' puddings.

Not one to leave things to chance, I engaged a company to conduct a feasibility study into the public's acceptance of such a concept, using focus groups. Unfortunately, we discovered that it was thought by many to be too restrictive, and we therefore adapted it to include starters (appetisers) and non-pie main courses as well.

English food – properly prepared – had always been a love of mine, though when I was younger it would have taken a lot to convince me that much of it had not been invented purely to torture young children. Those dreaded words, 'Look what you've got today for pudding, lucky you. It's junket (or semolina or tapioca).' They were all puddings that seemed to me to be served only when, curiously, my parents were absent for some reason and, if not eaten at the time, would even reappear cold at tea. And at my preparatory school, they somehow managed to perfect the technique of creating a totally tasteless stew: thin, with grease floating temptingly on the top. It really was absolutely awful, and adding salt merely turned it into horrible sea water instead.

So what was I to call this restaurant that was going to transform the image of real English food into something popular and accessible for families on an eating-out budget? Many permutations were put forward, until the very simple suggestion 'Porters' met with unanimous approval, especially because of the proximity of Covent Garden Market. We also had to launch the restaurant successfully, since it looked as if finishing off the conversion of the old market was going to be delayed for some time, certainly until well after Porters would commence trading (eventually, it reopened exactly one year after Porters). As a result the area was a bit quiet and not enormously tempting either, given the amount of work that was going on there.

In my view, the only time you can promote a restaurant successfully is when it opens and therefore we devoted consideration to both press and radio advertising and an active PR campaign. Fortuitously, we had an advertising company called Colmans next door, so we approached two young, highly creative copywriters there and suggested that they might like to consider a bit of moonlighting as we really could not afford to spend a fortune. Happily, they agreed.

Their first idea was based around Noël Coward's songs, but with a slight twist, like: 'There's good food just around the corner' and 'Don't you think that Porters is the rage, Mrs Worthington?' But in our view their absolute crowning glory was 'Porters for Englishmen', which was set to the tune of 'Mad Dogs and Englishmen':

> Porters for Englishmen
> The best restaurant bar none
> In London's Covent Garden
> We have, do beg our pardon
> The Ceylonese have recipes
> To send you on the run
> The Americans expect to eject you
> In sixty seconds
> The French are nice
> If you pay the price
> Of a very tidy sum
> With a Cypriot Greek

> You have to speak
> Two languages in one
> But Porters for Englishmen
> The best restaurant bar none
> Porters of Covent Garden – what an English
>   restaurant oughter.

Even performed by me it had all and sundry falling around laughing. The song was definitely what we wanted, as it would get everybody talking. Until we checked with the Noël Coward Estate – and even though the appropriate amount of silver would cross their hands, sadly they would not allow his songs to be bastardised in this way.

So it was back to the drawing board and idea number two. We used the song 'Yes, we have no bananas' but with a 'No' instead of the 'Yes'. The idea was that we used apples, rhubarb, pears and many other kinds of fruit that grow in this country and are therefore suitable for an English restaurant to offer, but obviously not bananas. We planned to announce why we weren't serving bananas on the day before we opened, building up to a daft sort of climax, as hopefully the campaign would make people start asking each other, 'Why *don't* they serve bananas?' Naturally, given our previous track record, once again we discovered that we could not use the song! Finally, we fell back on 'Our Porter's reporter outside Porters English Restaurant', with the great character actress Miriam Margolyes as our Porters reporter. She and I mobbed it all up. It was great fun, but without the impact of the first two, quite brilliant ideas.

At the same time our advertisement team put together a 'Count Down to Opening' campaign for London's *Evening Standard*. It was really simple, just a picture of a hot, steaming pie with a caption underneath, such as 'A Stately Plateful' or 'Peer Among Pies', and an opening date with the address and contact telephone number. While all this was going on, we were frantically trying to get ready to open, create other publicity, train staff, get the builders out of the way, and do all the million and one things that never seem to come together until the last minute – when, fortunately, they do. And so Porters was born, on 19 June 1979.

It would be wonderful to say that everything was perfect right from the start, and that we were packed to the rafters . . . however, the restaurant did get off to an acceptable first year. We built trade from quite a busy opening week, got decent reviews – most of the time – and operationally everything settled down reasonably quickly. A year later, Covent Garden Market reopened and we were completely swamped with business. Our footfall (customers walking in off the street) went up over 60 per cent in the first week. And it didn't stop there, because we got used to working at a quicker pace and, as we learned how to speed everything up, we were able to get even more customers through the doors. As a consequence of the level of trade, we decided to drastically alter the menu, going for exactly what the advertising focus groups had apparently told us wouldn't work – all pies and puddings – and within a short time we didn't look back, as everything was massively simplified. Some days we were doing over 1,000 customers – absolutely unbelievable and a huge success.

Unfortunately, some of our dishes simply hadn't worked, the most memorable being the wonderful-sounding Goose and Gooseberry Pie. It didn't appeal to our clientele and, once we discovered that there is very little actual meat on a goose, just a lot of bone and fat, we realised that the costings were terrible also. Duck and Black Cherry Pie went the same way. Other dishes, some of them quite surprisingly, never achieved sales levels high enough to justify keeping them on the menu. Sadly, among these were some particular favourites of mine, like Rice Pudding with Strawberry Jam, made with a little grated nutmeg and a blob of jam in the middle – quite delicious, the way that we wished mother had allowed at home. Also, Pear in Port Wine Jelly. And every time I see 'A bring back jelly campaign' in a newspaper, I want to inform them that you can try it by all means, but it simply won't sell in a restaurant. Strangely, the same is true of Treacle Tart: a bit of a shock, but maybe it's just too heavy and calorific.

Game dishes have never worked either, although maybe that is a reflection of the clientele that we attract, as Rules sell masses just around the corner. However, Game Pie, Dorset Jugged Venison and Venison Sausages all got the chop! Another problem has been that whenever we think up yet another wonderful-sounding soup, a few weeks later it is brought out by New Covent Garden Soup Company and is seen on the shelves of hundreds of supermarkets across Britain. Not that I am accusing them of plagiarism, and will admit to being slightly guilty of massive exaggeration, but we would literally cruise round the shelves of the local shops to check that any new soup was not already being produced by them.

The greatest mistake that any restaurant can make is to coast along thinking everything is working perfectly. Hopefully, we have never been guilty of that at Porters, even though there were difficult times, especially in the five years after 1981 when my much-loved father died at the comparatively young age of just sixty-nine. The sad consequence of this was a death duty bill of £8 million and eventually the loss of our wonderful family home – Weston Park in Shropshire, built by an ancestor of mine in 1671 – to a charitable foundation. During that period, much time was taken up in trying to sort out the future of Weston to ensure that the huge losses it had been making were stemmed. For this, a grateful government levied a further £1 million in interest from me.

Porters has altered a lot from those early days as we have adapted to circumstances, including changing the name to Porters English Restaurant, something deceptively simple that has reaped far-ranging and unexpected benefits, as you will find if you type the two words 'English restaurant' into Google. As the Internet did not even exist when we first became Porters English Restaurant, I cannot claim to have been thinking with prescience that far ahead of time. Instead, it was to shake off the tag line we had acquired of being 'that pie restaurant'. Many clever journalists would refer to me as 'Lord of the Pies', thinking they were the first to come up with that sobriquet, and it had stuck. However, Porters itself had moved on (even if the descriptions hadn't) to offer starters – a revolution, that – and non-pie main courses, in effect becoming a proper restaurant, more akin to how it was when we started, though still very reasonably priced.

During the 25 years that we have been running, there are two descriptions of English food and Porters that I have had to battle over continually. The first is that English food is 'bland', which I must admit it can be if it is not prepared properly. So much traditional English cooking involves lengthy and careful stewing or braising, tenderising the meat and bringing out the flavours. As long as the right ingredients and seasoning are used, there is no way that it should ever be considered bland, and certainly Porters' food never has been.

Some years ago, however, I was horrified to be alerted to a review in the *Big Issue* magazine describing our Steak and Kidney Pudding as bland. Apart from the fact that I could not believe that whoever had written the review had ever actually eaten one, it also happens to be a personal favourite of mine. What on earth could we do to correct that inaccurate description, and how could we accomplish it? We threw down the gauntlet to the magazine: allow us to invite people off the street to come in and have a free lunch, then ask them what they think about the place. Fortunately, the challenge was accepted.

The manager and I stood outside, feeling somewhat foolish, as one person after another refused our invitation of a free lunch. Clearly, they considered that there must be a catch, like having to sign up for life assurance or a charity donation. Finally we had four willing victims, who had a whale of a time and loved the food. Consequently, we had the most fantastic review from the *Big Issue*, who were quite gracious in stating that possibly their reviewer had got it wrong. One small battle won, the next one always approached very soon afterwards.

The second description is that Porters is a tourist place. Why is there always a strange assumption, particularly among the major food guides and restaurant reviewers, that English cuisine is only appreciated and consumed by visitors to this country? What absolute nonsense! The vast majority of our customers have been British to the core, and many have been coming since we first opened. Even top chefs in this country, who produce the most marvellous and inventive combinations of ingredients and dishes in their places of work, admit that when they get home all they really want to eat is good simple English cooking. Favourite choices are Roast Beef and Yorkshire Pudding and Rhubarb Crumble. Do the guides feel that *maybe* we are ashamed of English food? Every time Porters is described as a 'tourist' restaurant my teeth grate, my blood pressure rises and I feel that we will never win in changing the inaccurate perceptions of English food and the fact that the British, in their droves, actually love it.

At the front of Porters, right from the start, we have had a notice board listing the managers, with 'In' or 'Out' by their names. The Earl of Bradford is always at the top and unfortunately this gives a very clear indication to certain customers who want to push their luck a little. Many are the times that supposed 'great personal friends of mine' have either tried to jump the queue or get special treatment. Hopefully, I know the genuine ones enough to appreciate that they would never attempt anything like that. Over the years, the members of staff have got used to this and deal diplomatically, but firmly, with them. But I will never forget standing next to the board one day when two girls were leaving. As they passed it, one turned to the other and said, 'I wouldn't believe that if I was you,' pointing to my name with 'In' against it.

The other one answered, 'Why not?'

'He's in America.'

'How do you know that?'

The first girl responded triumphantly, 'Nigel Dempster said so.'

I pinched myself just to check, but Nigel Dempster (the former famous columnist of the *Daily Mail*) must have got it wrong for once, or maybe she had.

Some of the names of the dishes rather naturally give rise to misinterpretation and mirth: top of the list are Spotted Dick and Faggots. Unfortunately, every clever customer who makes a witty remark about either is merely the latest in a long line, but the waiting staff always behave politely as if this is the first time they have heard it. However, when our eighteenth birthday came along in 1997, I decided to give full rein to my frustrated desire to be a tabloid journalist and booked an advertisement for four nights in the *Evening Standard*. Each of these appeared as a newspaper headline:

> Do You Fancy a Faggot?
> Ever Had a Spotted Dick?
> Like a Little Roly Poly?
> Is Your Toad in a Hole?

We have enjoyed fewer comments since, but it did become a talking point and brought in a lot of customers! And now you can bring the whole Porters experience to your own table as you savour and sample our collection of recipes. Enjoy.

Richard, Earl of Bradford

INTRODUCTION

It's curious that many people who are eager to experiment with food and recipes from increasingly exotic climes and who are willing to track down weird and wonderful ingredients are inclined to dismiss traditional English cooking as nothing more than a motley collection of nondescript, stodgy dishes with quaint names.

The history of England is its cooking. Successive invaders to English shores, Roman, Viking and Norman, naturally introduced their own culinary traditions to the native cuisine. The returning Crusaders introduced Arab influences too, adding dried fruits and aromatic spices to both sweet and savoury dishes. Other costly, new and luxurious foodstuffs such as sugar, almonds and citrus fruits were also imported from exotic lands in vast quantities in the Middle Ages. Such foods became the newly fashionable status symbols of a rich and self-indulgent elite and were used lavishly in the great feasts of the time.

Many of these recipes have survived through the centuries, frequently undergoing intervention and adaptation to meet the tastes of a particular time. English cuisine is not static but continues to evolve and develop, incorporating new ingredients, ideas and cooking methods along the way.

What, then, happened to sully the reputation of England's splendid national cuisine?

The Victorians have a lot to answer for. Their huge, elaborate meals degenerated into stodgy, unappealing offerings, and cookery books of the time included countless recipes for rejuvenating the cold remains. Reheated mutton and overcooked soggy cabbage were mainstays of the middle classes. Eating for the most part had become a necessity to be endured rather than enjoyed.

Highly processed, commercial 'fast-food' versions of our once glorious dishes must also take a large part of the blame. Trifle, for instance, was in its heyday a glorious confection of soft, wine-soaked sponge, rich custard and fresh thick cream, whereas today's mass-produced equivalent is a lurid concoction of rubbery jelly (jello), overly sweet custard and synthetic cream packaged in small pots. Cottage Pie, once made with finely chopped beef, well-flavoured stock and creamy mashed potatoes, is now available frozen in a foil tray and consists of poor-quality, rubbery minced meat in strong dark 'gravy' topped with flavourless dried mashed potato. But when properly made, these dishes are superb.

The reputation of our once great national cuisine, which in the past was universally admired for the sheer diversity of its ingredients and imaginative cooking, deserves to be revived and restored to its former glory. Our traditional recipes should be national treasures. They have come down to us from the kitchens of the great aristocratic houses, humble cottages and city streets, where they were lovingly and skilfully created. We should cherish them as we would a piece of fine china or antique furniture. Such recipes are a valuable part of our heritage which is slowly but surely being forgotten . . . and if that is allowed to happen, it would truly be a tragedy.

STARTERS

The 'starter' before the main meal is small but sets the tone for the meal to come: light and tasty before a robust main course or filling and hearty before a lighter meal.

ASPARAGUS

Samuel Pepys wrote in his famous diary that he bought asparagus from an asparagus garden in seventeenth-century London. Battersea in south London was famous for its 'Battersea bundles' of 'sparrow grass' (the slang term for asparagus) and the City of London was ringed with asparagus growers, particularly in Deptford, Fulham, Isleworth and Mortlake. By the eighteenth century other areas had followed London's lead and asparagus-producing market gardens quickly sprang up.

In the past, asparagus was sent to market in bundles of 60 or 120 spears tied with osier twigs in traditional patterns to keep them firmly together. Twenty buds were put into a round and six rounds put together to make a hundred (120 buds). Although this practice has now almost disappeared, examples of the craft can still be found at the annual asparagus auction at the Fleece Inn at Bretforton, Worcestershire, in late May, where top-quality asparagus is sold. Carefully tied bundles are piled high on a long trestle table in the yard of the fifteenth-century inn for the auction, the proceeds of which go to the village brass band. Prestigious chefs from London and other parts of the country attend, as well as market traders.

The asparagus season traditionally starts in the first week of May (although, depending on the weather, it can start in mid-April) and lasts for just six weeks. Occasionally supplies are available slightly earlier than this in the south of the country owing to the milder climate. English asparagus is recognised has having the finest flavour in the world (the stems grow slowly in the British climate, enabling them to develop a much fuller flavour and fine, tender texture), so it is well worth waiting for!

Asparagus has always been a favourite of mine, as it is so versatile – just perfect as a simple starter, but wonderful in soups, salads or as a vegetable to accompany almost any plain dish. Personally I love it with a bit of mayonnaise rather than butter, but then I had never thought of adding orange before.

Many years ago I stayed on an asparagus farm in South Africa, where they specialised in producing it white for canning. This meant that it was back-breaking work, as every spear had to be cut off 15cm/6in below the ground, when just the tip was peeping through the soil. However, it also meant that anything that was well above the surface was considered to be wasted, and we were allowed to take as much as we liked. Cooked absolutely fresh from the field, it was a dinner fit for a king.

Bradford

ASPARAGUS WITH ORANGE BUTTER

When buying asparagus, look for spears that are fresh and green with compact, tightly closed, firm tips. Ideally asparagus should be eaten on the day of picking, but it can be kept wrapped in the refrigerator for up to 2 days.

Remove the thick tough part of the stem with a vegetable peeler. Rinse quickly under cold running water and cut off any damaged parts. There's absolutely no need to buy a special 'asparagus pan' to cook the vegetable. Put the asparagus into a frying pan and add just enough boiling water to cover. Add a pinch each of sugar and salt and cook for 2–15 minutes until tender but not soft – the actual time depends on the thickness of the stems. Drain very well – soggy, waterlogged asparagus is horrible!

225g/8oz asparagus
50g/2oz/½ stick butter
grated zest and juice of
*   1 unwaxed orange*

Trim and cook the asparagus as described above. Melt the butter in a pan and quickly stir in the orange zest and juice. Pour over the asparagus and serve immediately.

BREADED MUSHROOMS AND BLUE CHEESE DIP

These delicious crisp-coated mushrooms are a firm favourite on the menu at Porters.

36 chestnut mushrooms
2 tablespoons chopped fresh parsley
½ teaspoon dried mixed herbs
salt and freshly ground black pepper
175g/6oz/3 cups fresh white breadcrumbs
4 eggs
oil for frying

Wipe the mushrooms with a damp cloth, trim any large stalks and then pat dry with kitchen paper. Combine the parsley, dried herbs, salt and pepper with the breadcrumbs and place half on a large plate. Lightly beat 2 eggs in a shallow bowl. Dip the mushrooms, one at a time, into the beaten egg, and then roll in the seasoned crumbs. Place on a plate and chill for 20 minutes. Repeat the process with the remaining breadcrumbs and 2 eggs and chill for a further 30 minutes. Heat the oil in a deep-fat fryer to 190°C/375°F and fry the mushrooms in batches for about 5 minutes, turning them frequently with a slotted spoon, until they are crisp and golden brown. Drain on kitchen paper and keep warm while frying the remainder. Allow 6 mushrooms per portion and serve with creamy blue cheese dip.

BLUE CHEESE DIP

150g/5oz blue cheese, e.g. Stilton
6 tablespoons mayonnaise
2 tablespoons double (heavy) cream
3 tablespoons crème fraîche
50g/2oz cream cheese
pinch of salt and freshly ground black pepper

Crumble the blue cheese into a large mixing bowl. Add the remaining ingredients and beat together until thoroughly combined. Cover and chill until required. For a smoother result, place all ingredients in a food processor and blend for 45 seconds until smooth.

Mushrooms have been eaten in England since the time of the Romans, although the word 'mushroom' was first recorded in the fifteenth century and is probably derived from the French word *mousseron*.

CHICKEN LIVER, GARLIC AND BRANDY PÂTÉ

One of the simplest things to prepare, this is so often a disappointment. It needs to have all those ingredients that give it that extra 'oomph', like garlic, onion and herbs, plus it must be almost velvety smooth in texture rather than setting too hard.

This recipe might well be described as the super-deluxe version, with brandy and cream. Watch it being wolfed down and you will realise that those little extras can make all the difference.

Bradford

525g/17oz chicken livers
50g/2oz/½ stick butter
3 shallots, finely chopped
3 cloves garlic, finely chopped
3 tablespoons brandy
4–6 tablespoons double
*   (heavy) cream*
1 teaspoon chopped
*   fresh thyme*
salt and black pepper

Wipe the livers with damp kitchen paper and pat dry. Melt the butter in a frying pan. Add the shallots and garlic and cook over a low heat for 5 minutes. Increase the heat to medium, add the chicken livers and cook for 5 minutes, turning frequently. Add the brandy, increase the heat and cook for a further 3 minutes. Remove from the heat and allow to cool slightly. Transfer to a food processor, add 4 tablespoons of cream and the thyme and blend for 30 seconds. Season to taste and check the consistency, adding more cream if necessary. Divide the mixture between 6 ramekins and chill for at least 1 hour. Remove from the refrigerator 15 minutes before serving and serve with Melba toast or crusty bread.

Pâté is a French word that originally denoted a pastry case with a filling of meat, fish or vegetables. In England the term came to mean just the filling, baked in a dish until firm and usually served cold.

H E R R I N G

In the Middle Ages, poor people relied on stockfish (dried without salt) and salted and smoked herring. In fact herring became the staple stand-by for Lent and to satisfy the demand salted herrings were sent great distances, first by packhorse and later by cart. Large manor houses bought in extra supplies for their servants and tenants and enormous amounts were consumed. For instance, in 1334 Durham Priory alone bought 60,000 salted herrings!

The herring were gutted, salted or smoked and then packed in salt in barrels. Until the fourteenth century, Beaulieu Abbey had its own drying and kippering depot at Great Yarmouth. Red herrings were salted and smoked until they became hard, dry and reddish in colour. On fast days, when no meat was to be eaten, they were the most common food of the period for ordinary people, although it was reported at the time that eating them caused a terrible thirst.

Porter is a bitter dark beer similar to stout but with a hint of sweetness. It was first made in the eighteenth century as a cheap beer for working men, including porters – hence the name. After being unfashionable for many years, it enjoyed a revival in the 1970s and is now very popular once again.

PORTERED HERRINGS

Herrings are traditionally soused in malt vinegar, but try this mixture of wine vinegar, which has a lighter flavour, and porter, which gives the dish a wonderful deep, rich flavour.

2 bay leaves
4 fresh herrings, filleted
pinch of ground cloves
12 peppercorns
1 onion, sliced
150ml/5fl oz/generous ½ cup porter or dark stout
150ml/5fl oz/generous ½ cup white wine vinegar
1 teaspoon salt

Preheat the oven to 180°C/350°F/gas mark 4. Place half a bay leaf on each fillet and roll up the herrings. Pack them into an ovenproof dish in a single layer and sprinkle with the cloves and peppercorns. Arrange the onions on top and pour over the porter and vinegar. Sprinkle with salt and cover the dish with a lid or foil. Bake for 30–40 minutes. Leave in the liquid until cold.

Soused herrings are, in my view, one of the most underrated dishes, but when we put rollmops on the menu at Porters, they simply didn't sell at all.

Other countries, particularly in Scandinavia, boast a range of different kinds of pickled herrings, and shooting lunches in Denmark hardly ever consist of anything else – at least to start with. They're very tasty, plus doctors keep saying that oily fish like herring is extremely good for us and makes us live longer. So it's a mystery why the English don't take to them!

Bradford

SMOKED SALMON PÂTÉ

Smoked salmon is very rich so a little goes a long way. It has a particular affinity with good wholemeal (whole wheat) bread.

225g/8oz smoked salmon trimmings
juice of ½ lemon
50g/2oz/½ stick butter
2 teaspoons mayonnaise
1 teaspoon horseradish
3 tablespoons crème fraîche
pinch of cayenne pepper
1 teaspoon freshly chopped dill

Blend the salmon and lemon juice in a food processor. Melt the butter in a pan and slowly pour into the processor while continuing to blend. Add the rest of the ingredients until finely mixed but not over-blended. Spoon into 4–6 ramekins and chill until ready to serve.

POTTED   FOODS

When food was potted, careful preparation, cooking and preservation were essential to ensure that it remained fresh. The meat or fish was seasoned with salt and pepper, and flavoured with spices such as cloves, mace and nutmeg. Sometimes alcohol and/or lemon juice was also added. The mixture was then packed into pots, covered with butter and cooked at a high temperature to kill harmful organisms. Any that did remain were trapped in the thick layer of butter as it cooled and set. The top layer of butter also served to keep out dust and other contaminants. Ships' cooks had to ensure that provisions would last throughout long voyages, so much naval food was potted, pickled and highly spiced.

Strong, watertight, specially designed pots made from tin-glazed earthenware were created in which the food could be prepared, cooked and eaten. From the late nineteenth century pots were made of biscuitware and were often beautifully decorated and embellished by talented freelance artists. After use, empty pots were washed and became highly valued by the well-to-do as fashionable ornaments. They are now much-sought-after collectors' items in antiques shops.

POTTED SHRIMPS

This is traditional English food at its best. Top-quality, supremely fresh ingredients are flavoured with spices that enhance but do not overpower the flavour. The butter must not be too hot when coating the shrimps or they will become tough.

225g/8oz/2 sticks clarified butter*
¼ teaspoon ground mace
¼ teaspoon cayenne pepper
½ teaspoon freshly grated nutmeg
450g/1lb fresh boiled shrimps
salt

Melt half the clarified butter in a pan and then add the spices and shrimps. Stir well to ensure the shrimps are evenly coated in butter. Taste and add salt if necessary. Spoon the shrimps into pots and pour over the spiced butter from the pan. Press down well and leave until cold. Melt the rest of the clarified butter and pour over the shrimps to seal them. Chill in the refrigerator before serving.

To clarify butter, melt it over a low heat until the foaming subsides. Pour into a bowl and leave until cold. Carefully remove the top white layer, which contains the salt. Lift out the solid butter, discarding any liquid at the bottom of the bowl.

For me, these are simply the greatest English starter, but then, how many of you ever behaved with them as I did? When I was at Harrow School as a boarder, my favourite treat was to buy a pot of them and leave it to melt on the radiator before devouring the whole lot. That way you end up savouring that gorgeous buttery, nutty flavour – undoubtedly a wonderful way to make prep pass a little faster, even if there were sometimes some strange greasy marks on my essay paper when it was finally handed in.

Bradford

POTTED CHEESE

A fine farmhouse or craft-made cheese is by far
the best choice here – or indeed in any recipe that
calls for cheese.

225g/8oz cheese, e.g. Cheshire
50g/2oz/½ stick butter, softened
1 teaspoon Worcestershire sauce
¼ teaspoon grated nutmeg
3 tablespoons medium sherry
melted clarified butter to seal (page 30)

Grate the cheese and mix with the butter,
Worcestershire sauce and nutmeg until well
combined. Add the sherry and beat until it is
incorporated. Spoon into small pots or ramekins,
pressing down well. Smooth the tops, cover with
melted butter and store in the refrigerator until
needed. Remove an hour before serving. Serve
spread on bread, crackers or toast.

> Cheshire is believed to be England's oldest cheese. It is
> mentioned in the Domesday Book in the eleventh
> century, but probably predates the Roman conquest. The
> mellow flavour of this crumbly cows' milk cheese has a
> salty tang. White Cheshire is actually cream-coloured,
> red Cheshire was originally coloured with carrot juice
> but is now coloured with annatto (derived from a tropical
> plant) or beta carotene, and there is also a blue Cheshire.
> The latter is matured for longer than the other varieties
> and has an excellent slightly herbal, grassy flavour.

PORTERED STILTON

White Stilton has a sharp flavour, while the blue variety is more mellow, with a creamy texture. It's a matter of personal preference which one you use.

225g/8oz mature Stilton cheese
25g/1oz walnuts, chopped (optional)
75g/3oz/¾ stick unsalted butter
1–3 tablespoons full-flavoured porter or dark stout

Grate or crumble the Stilton into a bowl and add the walnuts, if using. Beat in half the butter. Add the porter a spoonful at a time, beating well until the mixture is soft and spreadable. Pack into pots. Melt the remaining butter and pour over the top to form a seal. Serve cold on crackers or bread. It can also be spread on bread and grilled until brown and bubbling. It will keep in the refrigerator for up to 2 weeks.

Stilton is the only English cheese to be legally protected and must be made in and around the counties of Leicestershire, Derbyshire and Nottinghamshire. In the eighteenth century the cheese – then known as Quenby – was sold at the Bell Inn, a coaching inn in the village of Stilton. Travellers became used to buying it there and over time its name changed to Stilton.

SOUPS

Originally soup was merely the liquor from a stew and the meat was served separately from the broth. The word 'soup' is derived from the 'sops' of bread put at the bottom of the dish to soak up or thicken the liquor.

SPICED PARSNIP AND APPLE SOUP

This is a speciality of my wife's, and we even serve it at mid-morning breaks for shooting parties at Weston Park.

Some people tend to look rather askance at the humble parsnip, as if to say, well, they grow below ground, we prefer posh vegetables that see the sunlight. But it is so versatile. It turns into a brilliant mash, is wonderful roasted and, for me, works best of all in soups.

Bradford

Cinnamon adds a delicate spiciness to this light soup. Increase the amount if you like a more pronounced flavour. Use eating apples that are not too sweet, such as Granny Smiths.

50g/2oz/½ stick butter
1 onion, finely chopped
5 parsnips, peeled and chopped
3 eating apples, peeled and chopped
salt and pepper
2 bay leaves
1.5 litres/2½ pints/6¼ cups milk or chicken stock (or
    a mixture of both)
½–1 teaspoon ground cinnamon

Heat the butter in a saucepan and cook the onion very gently until soft and transparent, but do not allow to brown. Add the parsnips and apples and season to taste. Cook for a few minutes, then add the bay leaves and milk or stock and bring to the boil. Reduce the heat and simmer gently for 25 minutes until the parsnips are soft. Discarding the bay leaves, place the soup in a food processor or blender and process until smooth. Alternatively push the mixture through a sieve. Return the soup to the pan and add cinnamon to taste. Adjust the seasoning if necessary and reheat just before serving.

For some unfathomable reason, continental Europe disdains parsnips. The Italians and French, for example, feed them only to their pigs. In England, however, parsnips have been enjoyed since the Middle Ages, when physicians credited them with curing toothache, stomach ache and dysentery. They have a distinctive flavour, which is enhanced by the addition of butter or cream, and a sprinkling of cinnamon, nutmeg or herbs.

WHITE ONION AND CIDER SOUP

The type of cider used here makes all the difference to the flavour. At Porters we favour Somerset apple cider. There are a few craft ciders made from single-variety apples which would also taste wonderful in this recipe.

75g/3oz/¾ stick butter
1 tablespoon oil
1.5kg/3lb 5oz Spanish (white) onions, peeled and
*   sliced*
bouquet garni, including 2 fresh sage leaves
salt and pepper
25g/1oz/¼ cup plain (all-purpose) flour
300ml/10fl oz/1¼ cups dry cider
1.5 litres/2½ pints/6¼ cups vegetable stock

Melt the butter and oil in a large pan. Add the onions, bouquet garni and seasoning and cook over a medium heat for 2–3 minutes. Reduce the heat and cook gently for 30 minutes, stirring occasionally. Stir in the flour and cook for 2 minutes. Add the cider and increase the heat until boiling. Add the stock and then bring to the boil once more. Reduce the heat and simmer for 30 minutes. Ladle 600ml/1 pint/2½ cups of soup into a blender or food processor. Allow to cool slightly, then blend until smooth and return to the pan. Check the seasoning and reheat gently.

If a completely smooth consistency is required, either repeat the blending process with the remaining soup or allow it to cool slightly in the pan and use a hand-blender.

Onions were introduced to England by the Romans and ever since then have remained firm favourites in English cuisine. They are included in any number of savoury dishes. In 25 years Porters has used more onions than Wimbledon has used tennis balls in the same number of championships!

BROWNED ONION, ALE AND CHEDDAR CHEESE SOUP

Brown ale imparts a slightly sweet, malty flavour to the soup, but you could also try using dark beer, which gives it more body. Either way, you will end up with a hearty, warming soup that makes for a real taste experience.

75g/3oz/½ stick butter
1 tablespoon oil
1.5kg/3lb 5oz onions, peeled and sliced
bouquet garni
salt and pepper
25g/1oz plain (all-purpose) flour
330ml/11fl oz/1¼ cups brown ale
1.5 litres/2½ pints/6¼ cups vegetable stock
150g/5oz mature Cheddar cheese

Melt the butter and oil in a large pan. Add the onions, bouquet garni and seasoning, and cook over a medium heat for 2–3 minutes. Reduce the heat, cover the pan and sweat the onions for 30 minutes, stirring occasionally. Remove the lid and cook uncovered for a further 20 minutes, stirring frequently until the onions are golden brown. Stir in the flour and cook for 3 minutes. Add the beer and increase the heat until boiling, then add the stock and bring to the boil once more. Reduce the heat and simmer for 30 minutes. Ladle 600ml/1 pint/2½ cups of soup into a blender or food processor, allow to cool slightly, then add the grated cheese and blend until smooth. Return to the pan and reheat gently. If a completely smooth consistency is required, either repeat this blending process with the remaining soup or allow the soup to cool slightly in the pan, add the cheese and blend with a hand blender.

CARROT AND GINGER SOUP

This vivid orange soup combines all the sweetness of carrots with the aromatic pungency of fresh ginger.

6 tablespoons butter
1 onion, finely chopped
2 cloves garlic, crushed
25g/1oz fresh root ginger, peeled and grated
1.5 litres/2½ pints/6¼ cups vegetable stock
150ml/5fl oz/generous ½ cup dry white wine
675g/1½lb carrots, peeled and chopped
2 tablespoons lemon juice
salt and pepper

Heat the butter in a saucepan and when hot add the onion, garlic and the ginger. Cook the onion gently until soft (about 15–20 minutes) but do not allow to brown. Add the stock, wine and carrots to the pan and bring to the boil. Reduce the heat and simmer gently until the carrots are tender – about 45 minutes. Transfer the mixture to a blender or food processor and process until smooth. Return to the pan and stir in the lemon juice and seasoning to taste.

Carrots were used in Tudor cookery, with new, improved varieties arriving from Holland in the reign of Elizabeth I. These carrots were yellow and purple, although the latter fell from favour. Orange carrots were also developed by the Dutch in the seventeenth century and in England the court of Charles I went carrot crazy, with the ladies of the court wearing fronds in their hair and also pinning the feathery leaves to their gowns.

TOMATOES

omatoes originated in Peru, where the plant grew in the wild, bearing fruits not much larger than a cherry. Spanish explorers brought tomatoes back to Spain and from there they were gradually introduced into the rest of Europe.

The Elizabethans called them as 'love apples' (a reference to their supposed aphrodisiac properties) and 'golden apples' – golden because the first tomatoes to reach our shores were not the familiar bright red variety we know today, but yellow.

Early botanists considered tomatoes poisonous, due to the fact that they belong to the Solanaceae family, along with deadly nightshade and belladonna. It's not surprising that tomatoes were regarded with great suspicion and were first grown as ornamental plants in sixteenth-century gardens. Even by the middle of the seventeenth century the tomato was still cultivated as a curiosity. The pungent odour of the leaves and bright colour of the fruit caused people to shun the tomato as unfit for human consumption and it was to be another 200 years before opinions changed.

The first mention of tomatoes being eaten in England comes in 1752, when Philip Miller wrote in his *Gardener's Dictionary*, 'in Soups they are not much used in England', adding that there were 'some persons who think them not wholesome from their great Moisture and Coldness and that the nourishment they afford must be bad'. They were always cooked for a long time to neutralise the toxins that were believed to be present.

Tomatoes only really became well known in the late nineteenth century, when they were regarded as a luxury. The cheapest were imported in barrels from America. Mrs Beeton described them as a 'Mexican vegetable', but botanically the tomato is really a fruit. Most nineteenth-century tomatoes were not smooth-skinned but were deeply ribbed and easy to divide into triangular segments. Many people still ate them as a fruit and the Victorians cooked them with sugar and made them into jam. Eating raw tomatoes didn't really take off until after the First World War.

ROAST TOMATO AND
BASIL SOUP

Use the reddest, ripest tomatoes you can find to make this delicious soup. The combination of basil and tomatoes is magical. To preserve its heady fragrance, cut basil into strips with kitchen scissors rather than chopping it with a knife.

675g/1½lb fresh tomatoes
salt and black pepper
3 tablespoons olive oil
25g/1oz/¼ stick butter
1 small onion, finely chopped
1 stick (stalk) celery, finely chopped
1 garlic clove, finely chopped
2 × 450g/1lb tins chopped tomatoes
3 tablespoons fresh basil cut into fine strips
600ml/1 pint/2½ cups vegetable stock
basil leaves to garnish
extra olive oil (optional)

Preheat the oven to 180°C/350°F/gas mark 4. Put the fresh tomatoes in a roasting tin (pan) and season with salt and pepper. Drizzle with 2 tablespoons olive oil and roast for 1½ hours. Cool slightly and blend in a food processor for 30 seconds. Heat the butter and remaining oil in a pan and add the onion, celery and garlic. Cover the pan and cook over a low heat for 5 minutes.

Add the roast and tinned tomatoes and 1 tablespoon basil and cook for 2 minutes. Add the stock, bring gently to the boil and then simmer, uncovered, for 30 minutes. Allow the soup to cool slightly and blend in a food processor for 1 minute. Add the remaining basil and process for a further 10 seconds. Return to the pan and reheat gently. Serve garnished with basil leaves and a swirl of olive oil if you like.

CAULIFLOWER, STILTON AND ALMOND SOUP

The Porters recipe for this smooth, creamy soup has the ingenious addition of a scattering of toasted flaked almonds.

25g/1oz/¼ stick butter
1 onion, finely chopped
1 clove garlic, crushed
1 stick (stalk) celery, finely chopped
1 small carrot, finely chopped
1 large head cauliflower, broken into florets
2 medium potatoes, finely diced
725ml/1¼ pints/3 cups vegetable stock
150ml/5fl oz/½ cup milk
150ml/5fl oz/½ cup double (heavy) cream
110g/4oz Stilton cheese
salt and black pepper
75g/3oz flaked almonds, lightly toasted

Melt the butter in a large pan, add the onion, garlic, celery and carrot. Cover and cook gently for 10 minutes, stirring occasionally. Add the cauliflower, potato and stock. Bring to the boil, reduce the heat and simmer for 30 minutes. Remove from the heat, cool slightly and blend in a food processor. Return the soup to the pan, add the milk, cream and Stilton, and heat through very gently. Check the seasoning and serve garnished with almonds.

The cauliflower was brought to England in the late sixteenth century. The earliest printed reference to it is in John Gerard's *Herball* of 1597, where it was given as 'cole florie'. Sometime during the seventeenth century 'florie' became 'flower', which then led to the name we use today.

LONDON PARTICULAR
PEA SOUP

This is a dense, grainy and satisfying soup that's a meal in itself. I use ham stock for extra flavour, but this can be salty, so check the seasoning carefully as you might not need to add any more salt.

900g/2lb split dried peas
50g/2oz/½ stick butter
50g/2oz streaky (slab) bacon, derinded and chopped
1 onion, chopped
1 carrot, chopped
1 litre/1¾ pints/4½ cups ham or vegetable stock
salt and pepper

Soak the peas in cold water for at least 2–3 hours. Melt the butter in a large saucepan. Add the bacon, onion and carrot, and cook for 10–15 minutes until beginning to soften. Stir in the peas and stock and bring to the boil. Cover and simmer for about 1 hour or until the peas are soft. Cool slightly, then purée in a blender or press through a sieve until smooth. Return to the pan, season to taste and reheat until piping hot.

Pea soup gave its name to the thick winter fogs once common in London (these disappeared with the introduction of smokeless fuels and the Clean Air Act): pea-soupers.

MAIN COURSES

In the early years of the twentieth century, society was fond of dining in clubs and restaurants. The future Edward VII, when he was Prince of Wales, had joined the gentleman's club White's, and similar establishments flourished. The food had an excellent reputation and included succulent joints, tasty fish dishes and delicious pies and puddings. Simpson's in the Strand began in 1818 as a venue for keen chess players, but its popularity was mainly due to the excellent quality of its meat, which was reputed to be the best in London.

ROAST BEEF AND HORSERADISH YORKSHIRE PUDDING

Porters' menu has a wonderful description of roast beef: 'Is to an Englishman's taste buds what "Land of Hope and Glory" is to his ears.' Its success depends on the quality of the beef – if it's bright red, then it hasn't been hung long enough to mature and won't have much flavour. Look for dark red, almost brown meat with yellowish fat to ensure maximum tenderness and flavour. Resting the meat afterwards is just as important as the cooking. It allows the muscle fibre to relax, which produces moist succulent meat.

1.8kg/4lb joint of sirloin on the bone
salt and pepper

Preheat the oven to 210°C/425°F/gas mark 7. Rub the meat with the salt and pepper, then place in a roasting tin (pan) and cook for 1–2 hours, basting from time to time with the juices from the tin. The exact time depends on how rare or well done you like your beef. Remove from the oven and allow to rest for about 20 minutes, kept warm, while you make the Yorkshire puddings.

HORSERADISH YORKSHIRE PUDDINGS

A new variation on an old favourite.

lard or beef dripping
175g/6oz/1¼ cups plain (all-purpose) flour
pinch of salt
2 eggs
300ml/10fl oz/1¼ cups milk
6 teaspoons creamed horseradish or horseradish sauce

Grease 6 Yorkshire pudding tins with lard or beef dripping and place in a hot oven, 210°C/ 400°F/gas mark 6, while you make the batter. Put the flour and salt in a mixing bowl and make a well in the centre. Break in the eggs and gradually work in the milk, beating until smooth. Remove the tins from the oven and place a teaspoon of creamed horseradish in each. Pour on the batter and cook for about 20 minutes until well risen and golden.

A dish created especially for Edward VII when he was Prince of Wales was a fillet of beef slit open and stuffed with foie gras and truffles, then sewn up and spread with butter before cooking. This extravagant dish was served with grated horseradish.

YORKSHIRE PUDDING

The first recipe for 'A Dripping Pudding' appeared in *The Whole Duty of Woman* by an anonymous author in 1737. The recipe stated that the batter of flour, eggs and milk should be placed underneath a joint of mutton, so that the meat juices could drip from the spit on to the pudding below. However, the recipe existed some time before its mention in print, as in the seventeenth century the same mixture was boiled in a pudding cloth.

The first recipe for Yorkshire Pudding by name was given by Hannah Glasse in *The Art of Cookery made Plain and Easy* in 1747. The pudding was served at Yorkshire coaching inns of the time, but with the advent of ovens in houses it could be baked in a tin or dish at home. The old recipes produced a pudding about 2.5cm/1in thick. It was – and still is – cheap to make and filling, so was often served before the main course to eke out a small joint of meat between a family. Any leftover pudding was enjoyed as a dessert with jam or syrup.

ROAST SHOULDER OF LAMB WITH ORANGE

This is adapted from Robert May's recipe (see below) for shoulder of mutton roasted with onions, parsley and oranges, which has a good balance of flavours. Nowadays mutton, although so tasty, is hard to find and so I've substituted lamb.

shoulder of lamb with the blade bone removed,
     approx. 2kg/4lb
2 tablespoons butter
365ml/12fl oz/1½ cups fresh orange juice
220ml/8fl oz/1 cup boiling water
few slices of orange

for the stuffing
50g/2oz/½ stick butter
4 onions, sliced
bunch of parsley, chopped
good pinch of grated nutmeg
salt

Preheat the oven to 190°C/375°F/gas mark 5. Make the stuffing next by melting the butter in a pan and add the onions. Cook very gently until they are soft and transparent but not brown. Remove from the heat and allow to cool, then add the parsley, nutmeg and salt to taste. Place the stuffing in the cavity left by the blade bone and secure with a metal skewer or tie with string. Spread the butter over the meat and place in a roasting tin (pan). Spoon over about a third of the orange juice, then transfer to the oven and roast, allowing 40 minutes per 450g/1lb plus another 15–20 minutes for well-done meat. Baste with the orange juice now and again during cooking. When the lamb is ready, place it on a serving plate and keep warm. Pour off the fat from the roasting tin and pour in the boiling water, remaining orange juice and orange slices. Bring to the boil, stirring, and simmer for 5 minutes. Season to taste and strain into a warmed jug. Serve with the lamb.

Robert May, the son of a master chef, was born in 1588. In his youth he spent five years training as a chef in Paris, followed by an apprenticeship in various London households of the gentry and nobility. Incredibly, his life spanned the reigns of Elizabeth I, James I, Charles I, Cromwell and Charles II. Around 1660 he wrote *The Accomplisht Cook*, a book which dealt solely with cooking and was aimed at middle-class households.

England at that time was affluent and people were eager to try new continental foods and cooking methods. *The Accomplisht Cook* showed much influence from Italy, France and Spain and also made more use of vegetables than previous cookery books had done. Although few quantities were specified in May's recipes, great care was taken with the amounts of seasoning. Instructions for preparing salads (the English were particularly fond of salads) and cooking sugar peas (new to England, developed by the Dutch) appeared in the book, along with many recipes using oranges, which had been a favourite in England since Elizabethan times.

LANCASHIRE HOT POT

900g/2lb potatoes, peeled and sliced
salt and pepper
900g/2lb mutton cutlets or middle neck lamb chops
450g/1lb onions, sliced
300ml/10fl oz/1¼ cups lamb or vegetable stock
25g/1oz/¼ stick butter

Preheat the oven to 170°C/325°F/gas mark 3. Place a layer of potatoes over the base of a greased deep ovenproof dish. Sprinkle with salt and pepper, then add a layer of meat and a layer of onions, seasoning each layer as you go. Continue layering the ingredients, ending with potatoes. Pour over the stock and dot the potatoes with the butter. Cover the dish and cook for about 2 hours until the meat is tender and the potatoes are cooked. Remove the lid, raise the oven temperature to 220°C/ 425°F/gas mark 7 and cook for a further 20 minutes in order to brown the potatoes. The finished dish shouldn't be as wet as a stew but just barely moist.

THE STORY OF LANCASHIRE HOT POT

The famous Lancashire Hot Pot gets its name from the pot in which it was cooked. These pots were sometimes called pipkins and were usually white or brown in colour and very deep. The basic ingredients consisted of mutton, potatoes and onions, although, as with all regional recipes, variations occurred depending on what was available the time. In the nineteenth century a few oysters were sometimes included, as they were very cheap and a staple food of the poor.

Pennine sheep are a lithe and hardy breed. Their long, straight bones were ideal for standing upright around the sides of the pipkin, with the other ingredients layered in the centre of the dish. Mutton was the meat most often eaten in the north of England. Lamb was almost never used – it was a rare luxury, available only as the result of an accident. Until the beginning of the nineteenth century sheep were valued for their wool rather than their meat and were slaughtered only when they had ceased to produce good-quality fleeces.

CITRUS PORK

This is best prepared the night before so the pork absorbs the citrus flavours.

2kg/4lb boneless leg of pork
juice of 1 large orange, plus extra if needed
juice of 1 lime
juice of 1 small lemon
2 teaspoons oil
2 cloves garlic, chopped finely
1 tablespoon fresh marjoram, chopped
2 sprigs fresh sage
salt and pepper
2 large onions, sliced

Marinate the meat for at least 2 hours but preferably overnight in the fruit juices. Preheat the oven to 180°C/350°F/gas mark 4. Process (or use a pestle and mortar) the oil, garlic, marjoram, sage and salt and pepper to make a paste. Drain the pork, reserving the marinade. Rub the paste all over the pork. Put the sliced onions in a roasting tin (pan) and sprinkle lightly with salt and pepper. Put the meat on top of the onions and pour the reserved marinade around (not over) the pork. Cook for about 2½ hours until well done (pork must not be undercooked) and the juices run clear with no hint of pink. If the contents become too dry, add more orange juice.

Rest for 15 minutes before carving. Drain the fat from the pan juices, then put the juices and onions in a food processor and blend to a smooth sauce. Slice the pork into thick rounds and spoon the sauce over the meat.

Pork has been enjoyed in England since ancient times. After the Norman Conquest there were plenty of pigs in England and references in the Domesday Book mention 'woodland for swine'. Pork was spit-roasted or cooked on a gridiron before the fire. It used to be said that pork could be eaten when there was an 'r' in the month, but since refrigeration it can be enjoyed all year round.

BRAISED FAGGOTS

Strangely, the name of this dish seems to cause much amusement among visitors to Porters from North America – not that we've ever managed to work out why! You can substitute 110g/4oz of both meats with roughly chopped lamb's liver, which, although traditional, is not as popular.

450g/1lb minced (ground) beef
450g/1lb minced (ground) pork
1 medium onion, finely chopped
1 medium carrot, finely chopped
2 sticks (stalks) celery, finely chopped
1 tablespoon chopped fresh parsley
1 dessertspoon chopped fresh thyme
1 dessertspoon chopped fresh sage
1 teaspoon tomato purée
2 cloves garlic, crushed
110g/4oz/½ cup shredded suet (shortening)
5 slices white bread, crushed to crumbs
salt and pepper
Onion and Ale Gravy (see below)

Preheat the oven to 180°C/350°F/gas mark 4. With the exception of the gravy, thoroughly mix all the ingredients in a large bowl. Carefully mould spheres between the size of a golf and a tennis ball – there should be enough for approximately 4 per person. Place the balls in a deep baking tray and three-quarters cover with gravy. Put tin foil over the tray and cook in the middle of the oven for 2 hours. When done, they should be firm if pressed. Faggots are best served with mashed potatoes, Onion and Ale Gravy and English mustard.

ONION AND ALE GRAVY

Porters has made enough onion gravy to paint the Millennium Dome six times!

50g/2oz/½ stick butter
675g/1½lb onions, half diced and half sliced
1 level tablespoon plain (all-purpose) flour
300ml/10fl oz/1¼ cups ale
600ml/1 pint/2½ cups beef stock
1 bay leaf
salt and pepper

Melt the butter in a large pan. Add the onions and cook over a moderate heat for 5 minutes. Reduce the heat and continue to cook for 20 minutes, stirring occasionally. Sprinkle the flour over the onions and cook for 2 minutes, stirring continuously. Gradually stir in the ale, increase the heat and bring to the boil. Add the stock, bay leaf and seasoning. Return to the boil, then simmer for 5 minutes.

LAVENDER HONEY AND CIDER-GLAZED ROAST CHICKEN

Avoid lavender flowers that have been sprayed with insecticide. To prepare the flowers, gently shake the stems to dislodge any insects before washing and drying carefully and thoroughly. Use kitchen paper to dry the flowers immediately after washing to preserve the fragrance. Only a few flowers are necessary to impart their heady scent – too many will give a bitter flavour to food. You can use fresh or dried lavender, although fresh lavender is actually stronger than dried. Alternatively you can buy culinary-grade lavender from herbalists.

3 tablespoons lavender honey
½ teaspoon lavender flowers (optional)
salt and pepper
1.5 kg/3lb chicken
300ml/10fl oz/1¼ cups medium cider

Preheat the oven to 190°C/375°F/gas mark 5. Combine the honey, lavender flowers and a generous sprinkling of salt and pepper. Spread the mixture over the chicken and place in a baking dish or roasting tin (pan) and cook for 40 minutes. Warm the cider and pour over the chicken, then cook for another 50–60 minutes until the chicken juices run clear when you stick a skewer into the leg. Cover with foil if it becomes too dark during cooking. Remove the chicken from the oven and leave to rest for 10 minutes while you make the glaze. Drain the juices from the baking dish into a pan and bring to the boil. Boil for 10–15 minutes until thick. Place the chicken on a serving dish and pour over the glaze. Serve immediately.

L A V E N D E R

The refreshingly scented deep-mauve flowers of the lavender plant were used extensively in kitchens in the past to add both flavour and colour to a variety of sweet and savoury dishes. In his famous *Herball* of 1597 John Gerard stated, 'the young and tender sproutings are kept in pickle and reserved to be eaten with meat'. Lavender flowers were scattered over the tables at medieval feasts to sharpen appetites as well as to perfume the air.

Lavender is also good with lamb – in fact, the French graze their lambs in lavender fields whenever possible so that the meat develops a unique, elusive flavour. A few lavender flowers and a sprig of rosemary scattered over a leg of lamb before roasting impart an intriguing flavour. Lavender is good for the digestion too, as it aids the flow of bile.

We can thank Queen Elizabeth I (who spent lavishly on her favourite lavender water) for the extensive cultivation of lavender in England. She was also reputed to have drunk copious amounts of lavender tea to alleviate her frequent migraines.

CHARGRILLED CITRUS-MARINATED CHICKEN

If you can, use the highly scented juice and zest from Seville oranges in this recipe. Their aromatic peel and astringent juice add a delicious tang to the finished dish. They have a very short season, from the end of December to the end of February, but can be frozen (whole and well wrapped) successfully.

finely grated zest and juice of 1 orange
finely grated zest and juice of 1 lemon
finely grated zest and juice of 1 lime
2 tablespoons sunflower oil, plus extra for cooking
½ teaspoon each salt and pepper
4 boneless chicken breasts, skin on
1–2 tablespoons plain (all-purpose) flour

Mix the fruit zests and juices with the sunflower oil, salt and pepper in a bowl large enough to fit the chicken breasts. Score the chicken diagonally with a knife, making shallow cuts. Put the chicken into the marinade and cover the bowl. Chill overnight, stirring occasionally. Remove from the refrigerator and allow the chicken to come to room temperature. Pat the meat dry and lightly dredge with flour. Heat a little oil in a frying pan and cook, turning frequently, until the skin is crisp and the chicken is cooked through. Remove from the pan and serve immediately.

The very first oranges to reach British shores arrived on a Spanish ship at Portsmouth in 1289 for Queen Eleanor, the Spanish wife of Edward I. These first precious oranges were costly and quickly became a status symbol, destined for the tables of the wealthy nobility. Sweet oranges were unknown in England until the fifteenth century, when they were imported from Portugal and China. The first orange trees in England are said to been grown by Sir Francis Carew in 1568. Samuel Pepys grew oranges in a garden in 1666. Early English cookery books (up to the nineteenth century) meant Seville oranges whenever oranges were required in a recipe. If sweet oranges were to be used they were described as 'China' or 'Portugal' oranges.

MINT-AND-APRICOT-GLAZED DUCK BREASTS

This is a marvellous combination of flavours, with the fruity apricots, sweet honey, lively mint and tart wine vinegar a perfect match for the rich, fatty duck meat.

4 duck breasts, skin on
salt and pepper
2 tablespoons olive oil
150ml/5fl oz/generous ½ cup wine vinegar
110g/4oz/¾ cup ready-to-eat dried apricots, roughly
    chopped
1 tablespoon honey
1 tablespoon chopped fresh mint

Score the skin of the duck breasts with a sharp knife in a criss-cross pattern. Rub with salt and pepper. Heat the oil in a frying pan, then add the  duck breasts, skin side up, and cook for 5–6 minutes until golden. Turn and cook the other side for 10–15 minutes until the flesh is just pink. Set the duck breasts to one side, keeping them warm. Remove the pan from the heat and drain off the fat. Pour the wine vinegar into the pan and add the apricots and honey.

Place over the heat and gently reduce by half.
Slice the duck breasts diagonally into 4–6 slices
and arrange on warmed plates. Pour the glaze
over the duck breasts, sprinkle with the mint and
serve immediately.

Jean Le Loup, gardener to King Henry VIII, introduced
the first apricots to England from Italy in 1542,
although some believe they were introduced earlier,
around 1524, by another of the King's gardeners. At
this time they were known as 'apricocks'. In
Elizabethan England they were grown on south-facing
walls in sheltered gardens in the southern part of the
country, but it wasn't until the eighteenth century that
they were cultivated with any real success. Apricots are
dried when they are fully ripe and are one of the most
successful dried fruits.

SALMON AND PRAWN FISHCAKES

At Porters the humble fishcake is transformed into a luxury gourmet dish and is served on a bed of spicy lentils.

350g/12oz salmon fillet
1 lemon, sliced
450g/1lb floury potatoes (Maris Piper)
2 tablespoons tomato ketchup (catsup)
1 tablespoon chopped parsley
1 tablespoon chopped dill
salt and black pepper
25g/1oz/¼ stick butter
2 shallots, finely chopped
175g/6oz cooked prawns
2 eggs, beaten
150g/5oz/2 generous cups fine white breadcrumbs
oil for shallow frying

Place the salmon in shallow ovenproof dish with the lemon slices on top and pour over enough boiling water to cover the fish. Allow to stand for 30 minutes. Boil the potatoes, then drain and mash with the ketchup, herbs and seasoning. Melt the butter in a pan, add the shallots and cook over a low heat for 5 minute. Stir into the mashed potatoes. Drain the salmon and flake. Roughly chop the prawns. Stir all the fish into the potato mixture. Shape the mixture into 12 patties. Dip in beaten egg and then breadcrumbs. Chill for 30 minutes. Repeat the crumbing process and chill for another 30 minutes or until you are ready to cook them. Heat the oil in a frying pan over a moderate heat and cook the fishcakes for 5–7 minutes on each side until golden brown.

GRILLED SALMON FILLET WITH BUTTERED FENNEL

If you can get it, use wild salmon here. The flavour is completely different from the farmed version, which has a softer, slightly flabbier texture than its wild relative.

4 fennel bulbs
salt and pepper
175g/6oz/1½ sticks butter
1 medium onion, finely chopped
squeeze of lemon juice
4 salmon steaks, each about 2.5cm/1in thick

Slice the fennel bulbs and place in a pan with a pinch of salt and just enough cold water to cover them. Bring to the boil and simmer for 10–15 minutes until just tender. Drain well. Melt 50g/2oz/½ stick butter in a frying pan and cook the onion until soft but not browned. Add the drained fennel and 50g/2oz/½ stick butter, and cook gently until the fennel is very tender. Season to taste with salt, pepper and lemon juice. Melt the remaining butter in a grill pan (broiler) under medium heat until foaming but not browned. Place the salmon steaks in the butter and turn them over so that both sides are coated, then grill on one side for 3 minutes. Turn the fish over and grill for another 6 minutes, basting with the

butter juices, until the fish is cooked through.
Serve immediately with the buttered fennel.

Salmon, nowadays much in demand, was once so
plentiful that, along with lobsters and oysters, it was
despised by the upper classes. As a cheap everyday
filler, it was eaten fresh, dried, sliced and pickled. In
1800 Thames salmon was widely regarded as the best,
followed by that from the Severn. However, by 1850
salmon in the Thames were virtually extinct thanks to
over-fishing and disease. Salmon are especially
vulnerable to pollution and clean, well-oxygenated
water is essential for spawning. By the beginning of the
twentieth century salmon was scarce and fast becoming
a luxury food for the wealthy.

PLAICE WITH WATERCRESS SAUCE

Its hot peppery flavour makes watercress the perfect foil for many different types of food, especially fish.

675g/1½lb plaice fillets
squeeze of lemon juice
salt and pepper
a little milk or water

for the sauce
300ml/10fl oz/1¼ cups chicken or vegetable stock
4 bunches or bags watercress
25g/1oz/¼ stick butter
2 bunches spring onions (scallions), white part only,
*   sliced*
2 tablespoons plain (all-purpose) flour
salt and pepper
4 tablespoons double (heavy) cream
1 tablespoon lemon juice

Preheat the oven to 180°C/350°F/gas mark 4. Put the plaice in a buttered ovenproof dish, then sprinkle with lemon juice, salt and pepper. Pour in the milk or water. Cover the dish and cook for 20–30 minutes until the fish is cooked through. Meanwhile, make the sauce. Heat the stock in a pan until boiling and add the watercress. Cover and cook for 5 minutes. Remove from the heat and leave to cool slightly. Melt the butter in another pan and cook the spring onions (scallions) for 2 minutes, then remove the pan from the heat and stir in the flour. Return to the heat and cook for 1 minute, stirring constantly. Pour the cooled watercress mixture into a food processor or blender and process until smooth. Return to the pan and stir in the spring onion mixture. Bring to the boil, stirring, then season to taste with salt and pepper. Remove from the heat and cool slightly. Stir in the cream and lemon juice. Place the fish on heated serving plates and pour the sauce over the fish.

WATERCRESS

Liquid pressed from watercress was sometimes included in verjuice – a tart liquid made from unripe grapes – until it was replaced by lemon juice when the Crusaders introduced lemons on their return from the East. Verjuice was used in cooking and as a condiment in the Middle Ages.

In England watercress was eaten mostly by the working classes, usually with bread but often on its own by those who were too poor to afford even a loaf. For this reason watercress became known as 'poor man's bread'. It was sold in Covent Garden and by London's street sellers, who tied it into bunches. Buyers ate the bunches from their hands, rather as we would eat an ice-cream cone. In Hungerford in Berkshire, a special Watercress Supper was held on the Monday after Easter. This consisted of Welsh rarebit, macaroni and watercress salad washed down with punch.

The plant once grew wild in streams throughout Britain and country people valued it highly, particularly in the winter months, when it was the only green leafy salad vegetable available. It wasn't until the nineteenth century that watercress farms were created in Kent, with beds running with pure, clear water. As the rail network improved, enabling fast transport, watercress was generally adopted into the diet at the same time.

John Gerard, the famous herbalist, praised watercress as a remedy for scurvy in the seventeenth century. Dr Nicholas Culpeper also extolled its virtues in *The Complet Herbal* of 1653: 'water-cress pottage is a good remedy to cleanse the blood in the spring, and help headaches and consume the gross humours winter has left behind; those that would live in health, may use it if they please; if they will not, I cannot help it. If any fancy not pottage, they may eat the herb as a salad.'

BEER-BATTERED FISH

Using beer and iced water produces the most
wonderfully light, crisp batter.

110g/4oz/1 cup self-raising (self-rising) flour
½ teaspoon salt
1 egg, beaten
150ml/5fl oz/generous ½ cup light beer or lager
        iced water
                6 skinned white-fish fillets, approx.
                175g/6oz each
                50g/2oz/½ cup flour seasoned
    with salt and pepper
oil or fat for deep-frying

Beat the flour and salt in a bowl with the egg. Stir
in the beer or lager gradually until you have a
smooth coating batter with the texture of double
(heavy) cream. If it's too thick add a little iced
water. Whisk well, then leave to stand for up to
an hour. Dip the fish fillets into the seasoned
flour. Heat the oil to 190°C/375°F or until a cube
of bread will turn crisp and brown in 1 minute.
Stir the batter and dip in a piece of fish, letting the
excess batter drip off. Carefully lower the fish
into the hot oil and cook for about 10 minutes
until crisp and golden, turning once. Don't cook
more than 2 pieces of fish at the same time or the

fat will cool down too much and the batter will become soggy. Drain on kitchen paper and keep warm while you cook the rest of the fish.

Fish and chips are a food marriage made in heaven! Fresh firm white fish enclosed in a crisp, light golden batter and tasty fried potatoes are traditionally served sprinkled with salt and vinegar. It's not clear when the combination first appeared. Fried fish was popular in Victorian London – there were over 200 fried fish sellers on the streets of London (Charles Dickens referred to a 'fried fish warehouse' in *Oliver Twist* in 1839) – although then it was sold accompanied by a piece of bread.

It's not definitely known when or where chips were first sold, or when they were teamed with fried fish, but Malin's of Bow in London's East End, which opened in 1860, is considered to be the oldest fish and chip shop in existence. The first fish and chip shop in the north of England is thought to have opened near Oldham, Lancashire, around 1863. The fish and chip trade spread throughout London and England's industrial towns (particularly in the north, where wives worked in the mills) to become a much loved national institution. Around 300 million portions of fish and chips are enjoyed every year in the UK, where there are now more than 8,000 fish and chip shops.

THE STORY
OF FISH

In the Middle Ages the Church decreed that more than half the days in the year were to be meatless. Salt fish, stockfish (dried without salt) and fresh fish from rivers, streams and ponds were a staple food for rich and poor alike. Fishmongers' guilds were created at this time – there was one for sellers of fresh fish and one for sellers of salt fish. Members of the fresh fish guild were not permitted to sell dried fish and were also forbidden by law to sell any fresh fish more than two days old. In London the Thames proved fresh fish, which was sold in markets (London's main fish market was Billingsgate, close to the river) and hawked on the streets of the capital.

People fortunate enough to live near the coast had a choice of fresh fish as well as shellfish. Freshwater fish were available to the wealthy, who had ponds and rivers on their lands. In medieval times, every monastery had its fish pond and these were good sources of pike, perch, trout and bream. Carp were introduced to England in the late fifteenth century and became very popular, as they were easy to feed and also grew well.

Many ingenious recipes for fish dishes were created. All types of fish were poached or baked with a variety of spices and dried fruits, baked in pies, stewed in pottages, masked with a tasty sauce or turned into brightly coloured jellies. Jellied eels are a surviving reminder of earlier times. Eel Pie Island near Richmond on the Thames gets it name from the famous pies served there. Visitors came from far and wide to savour the eels caught in the river and to debate if the pies were best hot or cold.

CAULIFLOWER, POTATO AND CHEESE LOAF

A twist on the traditional cauliflower cheese, you can serve this as a main dish with perhaps another vegetable or as an accompaniment to roast meats. It's particularly good with roast beef.

250g/9oz cauliflower florets
700g/1¾lb cooked potatoes
50g/2oz/½ stick butter
pinch of cayenne pepper
salt and pepper
4 eggs
150g/5oz/1½ cups strong-flavoured cheese, e.g.
    mature Cheddar, grated

Preheat the oven to 180°C/350°F/gas mark 4. Cook the florets in simmering water for about 10–15 minutes until tender. Drain and put into a bowl with the potatoes, butter, cayenne and a good shake of salt and pepper. Mash to a purée, then add the eggs, one at a time, beating well after each addition. Stir in 110g/4oz cheese and spoon the mixture into a well-greased loaf tin. Cover with foil and place in a roasting tin (pan). Pour in enough hot water to come a third of the way up the loaf tin, then cook for about 1 hour. Remove from the oven and turn out on to a serving dish. Sprinkle the remaining cheese over the top and return to the oven for about 5 minutes, until the cheese has melted. Cut into slices to serve.

Having been brought to England in the late sixteenth century, the cauliflower became a popular vegetable. It was often served on a thick slice of toasted bread (to absorb any liquid seeping out) with cheese sauce.

SPICY LENTIL, BEAN AND VEGETABLE PIE

Another fabulous Porters special!

2 tablespoons vegetable oil
1 large onion, chopped
2 cloves of garlic, chopped
1 red pepper, deseeded and chopped
1 large potato, peeled and cut into 2.5cm/1in dice
1 carrot, peeled and cut into 1cm/½in dice
½ small butternut squash, peeled and cut into
  2.5cm/1in dice
1 small courgette (zucchini), sliced into 1cm/½in pieces
1 teaspoon ground coriander
1 teaspoon ground cumin
1 teaspoon ground turmeric
½ teaspoon ground cinnamon
½ teaspoon cayenne pepper
1 tablespoon tomato purée
110g/4oz/¾ cup Puy (dried green) lentils
1 × 400g/14oz tin chopped tomatoes
150ml/5fl oz/generous ½ cup light vegetable stock
1 × 420g/15oz tin kidney beans, drained and rinsed
225g/8oz puff pastry
1 beaten egg to glaze

Heat the oil in a large pan, add the onion and cook gently for 5 minutes. Add the garlic and red pepper and cook for a further 2 minutes. Add the potato, carrot, squash and courgette to the pan and cook for 2 minutes. Add the spices and mix thoroughly for 2 minutes to coat the vegetables. Add the tomato purée and cook for a further minute, stirring continuously. Add the lentils, chopped tomatoes and stock, bring to the boil, then reduce the heat and simmer for 30 minutes. Preheat the oven to 220°C/450°F/gas mark 7. Add the kidney beans and simmer for a further 20 minutes, adding extra stock if required. Transfer the mixture to a 1.2-litre/2-pint/5-cup pie dish. Roll out the pastry large enough to cover the dish and cover with the pastry lid. Brush with beaten egg and bake for 20–30 minutes until the pastry is risen and golden brown.

Puy lentils, from the Velay region of France, are regarded as the best of their kind by gourmets. They keep their shape after cooking and are useful for adding texture to dishes.

SAVOURY PIES AND PUDDINGS

'Gret Pyes', ornately embellished, often crenellated and turreted, with their pastry decorations painted with edible dyes, were popular at medieval feasts. Pies were often gilded, sometimes in a chequered design, with banners placed on top depicting the various coats of arms of the guests. 'Endoring' was the favoured method of 'gilding' pies and poultry. A mixture of beaten egg yolks, spices and saffron was painted on to the pie just before the end of the cooking time and then it was returned to the heat to set to a gleaming gold.

STEAK, GUINNESS AND MUSHROOM PIE

Still the all-time favourite pie at Porters! You might like to try substituting red wine for the Guinness for a change.

25g/1oz/¼ stick butter
2 medium onions, 1 finely chopped, 1 thinly sliced
675g/1½lb chuck steak, cut into 4cm/1½in cubes
50g/2oz/½ cup plain (all-purpose) flour seasoned
with salt and black pepper
1 dessertspoon sunflower oil
150ml/5fl oz/generous ½ cup
Guinness (Irish stout)
300ml/10fl oz/1¼ cups beef stock
bouquet garni
275g/10oz button mushrooms
275g/10oz puff pastry
beaten egg to glaze

Preheat the oven to 170°C/325°F/gas mark 3. Melt the butter in a casserole dish, add the onions and cook gently for 10 minutes until soft and golden brown. Remove from the dish and put to one side. Toss the steak in the seasoned flour, patting off excess. Add the oil to the casserole, increase the heat and brown the meat in batches of 6 or 8 cubes. Drain the excess oil from the casserole, then return the onions and steak, increase the heat and add the Guinness. Bring to the boil and continue to boil for 1 minute. Add the stock, bouquet garni, salt and pepper, return to boil, cover and then place in the oven for 1½ hours. Add the mushrooms and cook for a further 1–1½ hours or until the steak is extremely tender. Check the seasoning, remove the bouquet garni and allow to cool. For maximum flavour this process is best done the night before. Store in the refrigerator, but remove 1 hour before baking. When ready to cook the pie, preheat the oven to 220°C/425°F/gas mark 7. Spoon the steak mixture into a 1.2-litre/2-pint/5-cup pie dish. Roll out the pastry slightly larger than the pie dish. Moisten the rim of the dish and place the pastry on top, sealing the edges well. Cut away the excess pastry with a knife held horizontally and lightly cut into the sides of the pastry (knock up), which helps the pastry to rise. Brush with beaten egg and cook for 30–40 minutes until the pastry is crisp and golden brown.

A BRIEF HISTORY OF PIES

Pies were popular feast-day fare as they could be prepared in advance and were also tasty and nutritious. In the Middle Ages, meat pies were much in demand and every town had its pie makers as well as butchers and bakers. Every type of meat, game and poultry was baked into pies, and, following the medieval custom, they were highly spiced, sweetened with honey or sugar and contained dried fruits as well as meat or fish. The Tudors enjoyed 'joke' pies, which contained live birds that flew out when the pie was cut open.

At the coronation banquet of Henry VII, an enormous pie was carried in by four men and placed on the King's table. When he cut it open a flock of pigeons flew out, followed by a hunchbacked dwarf, to the amusement of everyone present.

Wealthy people enjoyed pies filled with turkey, chicken or game, while poorer persons made do with giblet pie or umble pie – the latter made with the entrails of calves, pigs or sheep, hence the saying 'to eat (h)umble pie'. By the Elizabethan era tastes had changed and the sweetening was frequently omitted. Fresh fruit such as apples and gooseberries some-times replaced dried varieties.

All types of pies were sold by pie men in taverns and on London's streets up until the middle of the nineteenth century, when the pie shops caused their gradual demise.

LAMB AND APRICOT PIE

50ml/2fl oz/¼ cup vegetable oil
1.5kg/3lb lamb, diced
675g/1½lb onions, chopped
pinch of salt and pepper
110g/4oz plain (all-purpose) flour
3 dessertspoons tomato purée
300ml/10fl oz lamb stock
500g/1lb 2oz tin apricot halves
2 dessertspoons mint sauce
275g/10oz shortcrust (pie) or puff pastry
beaten egg to glaze

Preheat the oven to 180°C/350°F/gas mark 4. Pour the oil into a large pan and place on a high heat. Fry the diced lamb until the meat is sealed. Reduce the heat and add the onions, salt and pepper. Cook until the onions have become transparent. Add the flour and tomato purée and cook for 4–5 minutes. Add the stock, bring to simmering point and cook until the meat is tender – the longer the better. Drain and add the apricots and mint sauce. Adjust seasoning as required. Transfer to a pie dish and cover with either shortcrust or puff pastry, trimming off any excess and pinching the edges so that the pastry adheres to the dish. Lightly brush with beaten egg, make half a dozen or so small incisions and cook for about 30 minutes until the pastry is crisp and golden brown.

BUCKINGHAM PIE

Prime beef and venison cooked in a rich sauce make this another firm Porters' favourite.

50 ml/2fl oz/¼ cup vegetable oil
675g/1½lb stewing steak, diced
675g/1½lb venison, diced
675g/1½lb onions, chopped
salt and pepper
110g/4oz/1 cup plain (all-purpose) flour
220ml/8fl oz/1 cup red wine
300ml/10fl oz/1¼ cups beef stock
175g/6oz/1 cup fresh redcurrants
175g/6 oz leeks, chopped
3 dessertspoons tomato purée
275g/10oz shortcrust (pie) or puff pastry
beaten egg to glaze

Preheat the oven to 180°C/350°F/gas mark 4.

Heat the oil in a large pan and brown the diced steak and venison in batches, until the meat is sealed. Reduce the heat and add the onions, salt and pepper. Cook until the onions become transparent. Add the flour, then the red wine, and cook for 4–5 minutes, stirring frequently. Add the stock and bring to simmering point. Cook on a low heat until the meat is tender. Drain and add the redcurrants and leeks, adjusting the seasoning to taste. Transfer to a pie dish and cover with either shortcrust or puff pastry, trimming off any excess and pinching the edges so that the pastry adheres to the dish. Lightly brush with the beaten egg, make half a dozen or so small incisions and cook for about 30 minutes until the pastry is crisp and golden brown.

FIDGETT PIE

Some versions of this traditional pie add sliced potatoes to the filling. The name of this pie is believed to be derived from 'fitched', meaning five-sided, referring to the original shape of the pie.

2 cooking (green) apples
25g/1oz/¼ stick butter
2 onions, chopped
675g/1½lb ham, lean bacon or gammon (ham)
*   chopped*
freshly grated nutmeg
salt and pepper
1 teaspoon golden granulated (milled golden cane)
*   sugar*
150ml/5fl oz/generous ½ cup cider, beer or stock
225g/8oz shortcrust (pie) pastry
beaten egg to glaze

Preheat the oven to 180°C/350°F/gas mark 4. Peel, core and slice the apples. Melt the butter in a pan and cook the apples and onions for a few minutes until soft but not browned. Layer the meat, apples and onions in a greased 1.2-litre/2-pint/5-cup pie dish, seasoning each layer with a sprinkling of nutmeg, salt, pepper and sugar. Pour over the cider or stock. Roll out the pastry and cover the pie dish. Glaze with beaten egg and bake for 40–45 minutes until the pastry is golden brown.

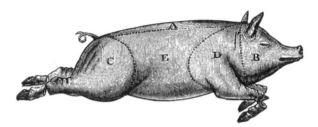

PORK AND LEEK PIE

225g/8oz leeks, sliced
450g/1lb lean boneless pork
salt and pepper
150ml/5fl oz/generous ½ cup milk
75ml/3fl oz/3 tablespoons single (light) cream
2 eggs, beaten
freshly grated nutmeg
275g/10oz puff pastry
beaten egg to glaze

Preheat the oven to 200°C/400°F/gas mark 6. Put the leeks into a pan and just cover with water. Bring to the boil and simmer for 5 minutes, then drain well. Cut the pork into cubes and put into a greased 1.2-litre/2-pint/5-cup pie dish with the leeks. Season to taste with salt and pepper. Pour in the milk and cover the dish. Cook for 1 hour. Blend the cream with the eggs and a little nutmeg. Remove the dish from the oven and pour in the cream mixture and leave to cool. Roll out the pastry about 5cm/2in wider than the dish and cover the dish, trimming off any excess and pinching the edges so that the pastry adheres to the dish. Flute the edges. Glaze with beaten egg and make a hole in the top of the pastry lid. Bake for 20–30 minutes until the pastry is crisp and golden.

CHICKEN, LEEK AND MUSHROOM PIE

A tasty combination of ingredients topped with crisp pastry.

50g/2oz/½ stick butter
1 leek, washed and
    sliced into
    1cm/½in
    rounds
275g/10oz chicken
    breast, cut into 2.5cm/1in cubes
225g/8oz chestnut mushrooms, wiped and cut in half
200ml/10fl oz/1¼ cups milk
150ml/5fl oz/generous ½ cup chicken stock
25g/1oz/¼ cup plain (all-purpose) flour
1 teaspoon chopped fresh thyme
salt and pepper
275g/10oz puff pastry
beaten egg to glaze

Preheat the oven to 220°C/425°F/gas mark 7. Melt 25g/1oz butter in a sauté pan. Add the leek pieces and cook gently for 5–8 minutes until just tender. Transfer to large mixing bowl. Increase the heat, add the chicken and sauté for 3 minutes. Add the mushrooms and cook over a high heat for 2 minutes, then reduce the heat and cook gently for a further 5 minutes. Add to the leeks.

Increase the heat, add the stock and boil for 1 minute to deglaze the pan. Allow to cool slightly and then combine with the milk. Melt 25g/1oz butter in a pan, stir in the flour and cook for 1 minute. Gradually add the stock mixture, stirring continuously to make a smooth white sauce. Add the thyme and cook gently for 5 minutes, stirring frequently. Season to taste, then gently combine the white sauce and chicken mixture. Transfer to 1.2-litre/2-pint/5-cup pie dish. Roll out the pastry slightly larger than the pie dish. Moisten the rim of the dish with water and then place the pastry on top, sealing the edges well. Remove excess pastry with a knife held horizontally and lightly cut into the sides of the pastry (knock up), which helps the pastry to rise. Brush with beaten egg and cook for 30–40 minutes until the pastry is crisp and golden brown.

Leeks are an ancient vegetable, one of the few mentioned in the first real English cookery book, *Forme of Cury* (*cury* was the Old English word for cooking, derived from the French *cuire*, meaning 'to cook, boil or grill'), which appeared in 1390. Here they were cooked with mushrooms and spices. They were popular in the seventeenth century, but after this seem to have almost disappeared from the tables of the well-to-do.

BEEF, MUSHROOM, CARROT AND ONION COBBLER WITH CHEESE-SCONE TOPPING

This satisfying pie is almost a complete meal in itself, although you can serve it with some green vegetables.

2 tablespoons oil or beef dripping
675g/1½lb stewing steak, diced
225g/8oz onions, roughly chopped
2 large carrots, sliced
300ml/10fl oz/1¼ cups beef
    stock, beer or red wine
1 tablespoon red wine vinegar
bouquet garni
salt and pepper
225g/8oz button mushrooms, halved

for the cheese-scone topping
450g/1lb/4 cups plain (all-purpose) flour
5 teaspoons baking powder
½ teaspoon English mustard powder
salt and pepper
110g/4oz/1 stick butter
225g/8oz/2 cups sharp-flavoured mature cheese, e.g.
    Cheddar, grated
2 tablespoons chopped fresh parsley
300ml/10fl oz/1¼ cups milk
beaten egg to glaze

Preheat the oven to 150°C/300°F/gas mark 2. Heat the oil in a flameproof casserole and seal the meat. Remove it from the pan and add the onions and carrots. Cook for a few minutes until lightly browned. Return the meat to the casserole with the stock, vinegar, bouquet garni, salt and pepper, and bring to the boil. Cover, transfer to the oven and cook for 1¾ hours. Add the mushrooms to the casserole and cook for another 45 minutes. Meanwhile, sift the flour, baking powder and mustard powder into a mixing bowl and add a good sprinkling of salt and pepper. Rub in the butter until the mixture resembles breadcrumbs, then add the cheese and parsley. Pour in the milk and knead lightly to form a soft dough. Wrap in cling film (plastic wrap) and chill for 30 minutes. Roll out on a lightly floured surface to 1cm/½in thickness. Cut into rounds and arrange on top of the casserole. Brush with beaten egg. Cook for about 25 minutes at 190°C/375°F/gas mark 5 until the topping is golden and risen.

A 'cobbler' is a later version of a pie which has this sort of savoury scone-dough topping.

LUXURY FISH PIE

The wonderful ingredients of this luxurious pie make it good enough to serve at a dinner party.

450g/1lb cod fillet, cut into 4cm/1½in cubes
225g/8oz salmon fillet, cubed
600ml/1 pint/2½ cups milk
2 bay leaves
10 whole peppercorns
900g/2lb potatoes
75g/3oz/¾ stick butter
salt and pepper
40g/1½oz/1½ tablespoons plain (all-purpose) flour
150ml/5fl oz/generous ½ cup double (heavy) cream
1 level tablespoon chopped parsley
½ tablespoon chopped dill
175g/6oz peeled cooked prawns
50g/2oz/½ cup grated Cheddar cheese

Preheat the oven to 200°C/400°F/gas mark 6. Place the cod and salmon in a deep ovenproof dish approximately 23cm/ 9in in diameter. Put the milk, the bay leaves and peppercorns in a saucepan, slowly bring to simmering point and then pour over the fish. Leave to stand for 20 minutes. Remove the bay leaves and peppercorns and then strain through a fine colander, reserving all the cooking liquid. Peel the potatoes and cut them in half. Place them in a pan of salted water, bring to the boil and cook for 15–20 minutes or until tender. Drain and mash with 25g/1oz butter, season with pepper and then place over a low heat and beat with a wooden spoon for 2–3 minutes. Set aside. Melt 50g/2oz butter in a pan, stir in the flour and cook for 1 minute. Gradually stir in the reserved liquid to form a white sauce. Add cream, parsley, dill and seasoning, and cook gently for 5 minutes, stirring frequently. Gently fold the cooked fish and prawns into the white sauce and then pour into an ovenproof dish. Spoon the mashed potato over the top of the fish mixture and sprinkle with grated cheese. Cook for 30–40 minutes or until golden brown and bubbling.

The humble potato was worshipped and revered in ancient Peru and was cultivated in South America for centuries before its discovery by Europeans in the sixteenth century. Its arrival in England was greeted with suspicion, hostility and even fear – not surprisingly, when you consider that potatoes belong to the same family (Solanaceae) as deadly nightshade and tobacco! But with the passing of time, the unattractive-looking vegetable gradually gained favour until, by the late eighteenth century, potatoes had become our staple food and the world's third most important crop.

CHEESE AND ONION PIE

A firm childhood favourite!

225g/8oz shortcrust (pie) pastry
2 onions, finely chopped
2 eggs, beaten
salt and pepper
freshly grated nutmeg
225g/8oz/2 cups grated mature farmhouse Cheddar
    cheese

Preheat the oven to 200°C/400°F/gas mark 6. Roll out two-thirds of the pastry and line a flan tin. Place the onions in a pan with just enough water to cover and bring to the boil. Simmer for 5 minutes, then remove from the heat and drain off the water. Allow to cool slightly, then beat in the eggs (reserving a little for the glaze) and season to taste with salt, pepper and nutmeg – be careful if using a salty cheese. Add the cheese and put the mixture into the pastry case. Roll out the rest of the pastry to form a lid. Dampen the edges of the pastry and place over the filling, pressing the edges well together to seal. Brush with the re-maining beaten egg. Bake for about 30 minutes until golden brown. Serve hot.

England has produced delicious cheeses for centuries and has built up a splendid tradition of superb regional varieties. In the Middle Ages cheeses were described according to texture rather than where they were made: for example, hard, soft or green. ('Green' referred to the newness of soft, moist, fresh curd cheese and not the colour – although sometimes herbs were added.) Gradually local cheeses became more widely known, especially at local cheese fairs. In the late seventeenth century London cheesemongers formed an unofficial guild, journeying throughout England to purchase cheeses from counties where they were made and sending them back to London by coach or river, where they were sold at a good profit.

HERB GARDEN PIE

A light summery dish, with a filling of delicious vegetables and fragrant herbs that vegetarians will love.

110g/4oz/1 cup garden peas
225g/8oz young carrots, thinly sliced
225g/8oz small courgettes (zucchini), thinly sliced
2 spring onions (scallions), thinly sliced
2 egg yolks
300ml/10fl oz/1¼ cups whipping or double (heavy)
    cream
1 sprig fresh tarragon, roughly chopped
½ tablespoon chopped fresh chervil
1 tablespoon chopped fresh lemon thyme or thyme
½ teaspoon each of salt and pepper
225g/8oz puff pastry
milk to glaze

Preheat the oven to 200°C/ 400°F/gas mark 6. Place the vegetables in a buttered shallow ovenproof baking dish. Beat the egg yolks with the cream, herbs and salt and pepper, and pour over the vegetables. Roll out the pastry so it is big enough to fit the top of the dish. Moisten the edges of the dish and lay the pastry on top, pressing the edges gently to seal. Brush the pie with a little milk and cut 2 small holes or slits in the top to allow the steam to escape. Bake for about 30 minutes until the pastry is puffed and golden.

Tarragon has a delicate liquorice flavour and is particularly delicious when used with summer vegetables. The herb is first mentioned in England in 1538 by Sir Thomas Elyot in his *Dictionary*, where he describes it as tasting like ginger. It was grown in the royal gardens in the Tudor period. Chervil is a member of the parsley family and has a slight aniseed flavour. It was probably brought to Britain by the Romans and was much used in the cookery of the fifteenth and sixteenth centuries.

STEAK AND KIDNEY PUDDING

Cockneys call the pudding affectionately 'Kate and Sydney Pudding'. It is one of the triumphs of English cuisine.

25g/1oz/¼ stick butter
1 large onion, finely chopped
675g/1½lb chuck steak, cut into 4cm/1¼in cubes
50g/2oz/½ cup plain (all-purpose) flour seasoned
*   with salt and pepper*
225g/8oz ox kidney, half chopped finely, half cut into
*   2.5cm/1in cubes*
600ml/1 pint/2½ cups beef stock
2 bay leaves
275g/10oz/2¼ cups self-raising (self-rising) flour
½ teaspoon salt
150g/5oz/generous ½ cup beef suet (shortening)
300ml/10fl oz/1¼ cups water

Preheat the oven to 170°C/325°F/gas mark 3. Melt the butter in a large ovenproof casserole, add the onion and cook over a low heat for 5 minutes. Toss the steak in the seasoned flour and pat off any excess. Increase the heat and add the steak to the onions in the casserole and sauté for 5 minutes until browned on all sides. Add the kidneys and cook for a further 2 minutes. Add the stock and bay leaves. Cover, transfer to the oven and cook for 2½–3 hours or until the steak is very tender. Check the seasoning and allow to cool. To make the pastry, sift the flour and salt into a mixing bowl. Stir in the shredded suet and then add water gradually, using a knife, until the dough is soft and elastic. Turn out on to a floured board and knead lightly for 2–3 minutes. Roll out three-quarters of the pastry into a circle large enough to line a greased 1.2-litre/2-pint/5-cup pudding basin. Line the basin, then, using a slotted spoon, fill with the steak and kidney mixture, pouring in enough cooking liquid to fill the basin two-thirds full. Keep any remaining liquid to use as gravy when serving the pudding. Roll out the remaining pastry to make a lid. Brush the edges of the pastry lid with water and then press on top of the pudding, sealing the edges well. Cover the basin with a large double sheet of foil with a pleat in the centre. Secure the foil with string. Place the basin in a steamer or a covered saucepan half-filled with simmering water and cook for 1 hour, topping up with boiling water when required. Carefully remove the basin from the pan and allow to rest for 15 minutes. Remove the foil and gently loosen pudding from the sides of basin using a palette knife. Turn out on to a serving dish and pour over the gravy.

THE FIRST PUDDINGS

The earliest puddings we know of, from around the time of the Norman invasion, were simply a mixture of spiced meat, often with cereal, packed into skins made from animal intestines. Pudding cloths were invented at the start of the seventeenth century: here the mixture was enclosed in the cloth and boiled. Puddings became part of the normal diet of almost everyone. They were easy to make because, once the ingredients were mixed and tied into the pudding cloth, they could be cooked alongside the meat in a pot over the fire. Different regions developed their own particular puddings using local ingredients. Savoury and sweet, boiled and baked, puddings formed a major part of eighteenth-century fare. Indeed, there were so many that visitors to England were amazed at the variety as well as the quality.

Suet puddings were popular in the nineteenth century and boiled meat or currant dumplings were sold on the streets of London in the early part of the century. Although originally regarded as a dish for the lower classes, by the end of the century puddings were considered acceptable fare at the great country houses.

Steak pudding was enjoyed in the eighteenth century and possibly before that. In *The Art of Cookery made Plain and Easy* of 1747 Hannah Glasse gave a recipe, as did Eliza Acton in her *Modern Cookery for Private Families* of 1845, although neither recipe mentions kidney. In her *Book of Household Management* of 1861 Mrs Beeton also gave a recipe for 'Steak and Kidney Pudding'.

The famous tavern 'Ye Old Cheshire Cheese' in Fleet Street issued an invitation to the opening of the 163rd Pudding Season at 7pm on 12th October 1930 for the serving of its famous pudding, the recipe for which was a closely guarded secret. The filling of steak, kidney, mushrooms and oysters, also included the unusual addition of plover and 'spices from ye far West Indies'.

BEEFSTEAK PUDDING

This recipe, adapted from Lady Clark's collection (see page 112), was from her cook, Mrs Wellington, and is slightly different from the usual beefsteak pudding as it contains ham.

450g/1lb/4 cups plain (all-purpose) flour plus 2
    tablespoons
225g/8oz/1 cup shredded suet (shortening)
salt and pepper
675g/1½lb shin beef or stewing steak, diced
225g/8oz ham, diced
1–2 shallots, chopped finely
½ teaspoon mushroom ketchup (catsup)
beef stock

Stir together the flour, suet and a pinch of salt, and add enough cold water to form a soft but not sticky dough. Roll out two-thirds of the dough and line a greased pudding basin. Place 2 table-spoons flour on a plate and mix in salt and pepper to taste. Roll the diced meat in this, then place in the lined pudding basin. Sprinkle in the shallots and the ketchup. Pour in sufficient beef stock to come three-quarters of the way up the meat. Roll out the remaining pastry to make a lid and cover the meat, sealing the edges well. Cover the basin with a lid (allowing for expansion during cooking) or greaseproof paper pleated in the middle, then a double thickness of foil pleated in the middle, and tie securely. Place in a large pan with enough boiling water to come halfway up the sides of the basin and cook for 4½ hours, topping up with boiling water as needed. Remove the basin from the pan, allow to stand for a few minutes, then turn out on to a hot plate and serve.

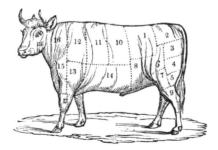

LADY CLARK OF TILLYPRONIE

*T*he *Cookery Book of Lady Clark of Tillypronie* was published in 1909, after her death, and was a collection of recipes scribbled down by her during her lifetime. Lady Clark had a passion for cooking and was a voracious reader and collector of recipes. She wrote the recipes on the backs of envelopes, scraps of paper, old bills and along the margins of cookery books. None of the recipes was from printed sources; instead she gleaned them from servants, friends and acquaintances.

Lady Clark, the daughter of a judge, was the wife of Lord Clark, who was in the Diplomatic Service. They lived at various times at Tillypronie, Birk Hall and Bagshot Park. She was a celebrated hostess, known for her wit and intelligence, and was unusual for the time in that she enjoyed discussing food in an age when it was considered ill bred to comment on the cooking at table. Her husband, though, didn't share her culinary enthusiasm; in fact he thought it rather distasteful. However, this did not deter Lady Clark, whose collection of recipes is delightful and includes those from the nobility, such as the Oyster Quenelles from the Duke of Devonshire, recipes from chefs and cooks of the great houses of the day and also from French émigrés (including Louis XVIII, a renowned gourmet) whom she met as a girl.

CHICKEN, HAM AND PARSLEY PUDDING

A combination of tasty ingredients enclosed in a parsley-flecked suet crust.

for the suet crust
450g/1lb self-raising (self rising) flour
225g/8oz/1 cup shredded suet (shortening)
1 teaspoon salt
4 tablespoons chopped fresh parsley
water to mix

for the filling
450g/1lb boneless chicken breasts, cut into chunks
450g/1lb lean raw ham, roughly chopped
plain (all-purpose) flour seasoned with salt and
    pepper
2 onions, finely chopped
2 teaspoons chopped fresh thyme or sage leaves
chicken stock

First make the suet crust. Put the dry ingredients in a mixing bowl and add just enough water to make a firm dough. Turn out on to a floured board and knead lightly for 2–3 minutes. Roll out three-quarters into a circle large enough to line a greased 1.2-litre/2-pint/5-cup pudding basin. For the filling, dip the chicken and ham pieces into the seasoned flour. Put a layer of chicken and ham, followed by a layer of onions, into the basin, continuing until it is full. Sprinkle each layer with a little salt and pepper and a little of the chopped fresh herbs. Pour in just enough chicken stock to cover. Cover firmly with a suet crust lid made from the remaining pastry and seal the edges well. Steam as for Steak and Kidney Pudding (see page 106).

In fifteenth-century England 'Poddyng of Capoun necke' was prepared by the court cooks. The gizzard, heart and liver were chopped finely and bound with egg yolks. Spices were added and the mixture stuffed and sewn into an intestine before cooking.

SAUSAGE, BACON AND APPLE PUDDING

A tasty, filling autumn or winter dish. Vary the flavour by using thyme instead of sage. You can also use beer or red wine instead of the vegetable stock or cider.

for the suet crust
450g/1lb/4 cups self-raising (self-rising) flour
225g/8oz/1 cup shredded suet (shortening)
1 teaspoon salt
4 tablespoons chopped fresh parsley
water to mix

for the filling
900g/2lb lean pork sausage meat (from Porters
handmade sausages)
225g/8oz lean bacon, diced
1 large cooking (green) apple
1 onion, sliced
salt and pepper
2 teaspoons chopped fresh sage
150ml/5fl oz/1 generous ½ cup vegetable stock or dry
cider

First make the suet crust. Put the dry ingredients in a mixing bowl and add just enough water to make a firm dough. Roll out on a floured surface. Line a 1.2-litre/2-pint/5-cup pudding basin with two-thirds of the pastry. For the filling, place alternate layers of the sausage meat, bacon, apple and onion in the basin, seasoning each layer with salt, pepper and sage. Pour in the stock or cider and cover with a lid made from the remaining pastry. Steam as for Steak and Kidney Pudding (see page 106) for 2½ hours.

The pig-rearing regions of England developed many different recipes for savoury puddings using bacon, ham and pork. A pudding, with its hearty suet crust, was the ideal way to stretch a little meat a long way to feed a hungry family.

CHEESE PUDDING

This is an old-fashioned dish that has (unfairly) been relegated to oblivion. When it is properly made with top-quality ingredients, it is just as good as – if not better than – a cheese soufflé.

600ml/1 pint/2½ cups milk
50g/2oz/½ stick butter
110g/4oz/2 cups fresh wholemeal (whole wheat) or
*   granary breadcrumbs*
2 teaspoons made mustard
pinch of grated nutmeg
pinch of ground mace
pinch of cayenne pepper
salt
2 large eggs, separated
175g/6oz/1¼ cups Wensleydale cheese, crumbled

Heat the milk and butter and, when hot, add the breadcrumbs. Leave to stand for at least an hour. Preheat the oven to 200°C/400°F/gas mark 6. Add the mustard, spices, cayenne pepper and salt to the egg yolks and beat well. Stir into the breadcrumb mixture with the cheese. Whisk the egg whites until stiff but not dry and gently fold into the mixture. Pour into a buttered 1.5-litre/2½-pint/6½-cup pie dish and cook for about 40 minutes until risen and golden brown and the centre of the pudding is cooked.

THE STORY OF WENSLEYDALE CHEESE

Wensleydale is the most famous of all the Yorkshire Dale cheeses. Moist and crumbly with a mild sweet flavour, it's usually eaten when young. The recipe for Wensleydale can be traced back to the Cistercian monks, who came over to England with William the Conqueror in the eleventh century, bringing with them their cheese-making skills.

The monks held large tracts of land in the Dales and the Cistercians at Jervaulx made a blue-veined cheese with ewes' milk using the same methods as for Roquefort. Ewes' milk was used until about the fourteenth century, at which point cows' milk began to be used instead. It's reasonable to suppose that the reason for this was that it took much less time and effort to milk one cow than several sheep!

The Reformation during the reign of Henry VIII caused the monks to flee from persecution and seek refuge with local families. The grateful monks gave their secret recipe for the cheese to these families, who started to make it on their smallholdings and farms.

This small-scale production continued until the end of the nineteenth century, but was almost facing extinction when the first creamery was opened in Hawes, North Yorkshire, by Edward Chapman, a corn and provisions merchant in the town, in 1897. He began to purchase milk from the surrounding farms to use in the manufacture of Wensleydale cheese on a larger scale. The invention of motor transport made the collection of milk from scattered farms in the area easier, so it was viable to produce cheese in large centres.

It wasn't until the nineteenth century that the cheese acquired the name Wensleydale and it remained a blue-veined cheese until the 1920s, when changes in the production methods caused the veining to disappear and led to the creation of the now familiar white cheese. Recently, by following ancient traditional recipes, blue Wensleydale has been revived.

SWEET PUDDINGS AND DESSERTS

English puddings and desserts (known in the past as 'conceited dishes') were once admired throughout the world. The English are renowned for their 'sweet tooth' and nowhere is this more in evidence than in the huge variety of creams, custards, fools, mousses and jellies that have been popular for hundreds of years. Until the middle of the last century, cookery books regularly gave instructions for the making of elaborate confections of spun sugar into Chinese temples, pagodas and suchlike. At grand entertainments and banquets, a stunning centrepiece would be arranged on the table for guests to marvel at. One of these consisted of a desert island covered with a 'silver web' of spun sugar. Such extravagances have now disappeared, but the desserts of yesteryear remain as popular as ever.

Rich, creamy syllabubs, custards and trifles, together with the more substantial steamed and baked puddings, are peerless, as is the mouth-watering array of sweet and savoury pies, tarts and flans that have always been national favourites.

LADY BRADFORD'S STICKY GINGERBREAD PUDDING

A gloriously fragrant pudding much in demand at Porters – the diced apples and stem ginger make it ambrosial!

75g/3oz/¾ stick butter
150ml/5fl oz/generous ½ cup milk
1 tablespoon black treacle (molasses)
1 tablespoon golden (corn) syrup
1 egg
75g/3oz/½ cup dark muscovado (dark brown
*   molasses) sugar*
175g/6oz/1¼ cups self-raising (self-rising) flour
1 level teaspoon baking powder
1 level teaspoon bicarbonate of soda (baking soda)
2 level teaspoons ground ginger
1 level teaspoon ground cinnamon
½ level teaspoon ground cloves
75g/3oz stem ginger, finely chopped
110g/4oz cooking (green) apples, peeled and finely
*   diced*

Place the butter, milk, treacle (molasses) and golden (corn) syrup in a pan and heat gently until the butter has melted. Allow to cool, then whisk in the egg and sugar. Sift the flour, baking powder, bicarbonate of soda (baking soda) and spices into a large mixing bowl. Make a well in

the centre of the dry ingredients and stir in the liquid to create a smooth batter. Fold in the stem ginger and apples, then pour into a buttered 1.2-litre/2-pint/5-cup pudding basin. Cover with a square of foil with a pleat in the centre and secure with string. Steam for 1½ hours or until the pudding springs back when pressed lightly. Turn out on to a serving plate and serve with custard.

This is just one of Lady Bradford's many specialities that I keep hoping, for the sake of my waistline, she won't make too often. Like Oscar Wilde, I can resist almost anything except temptation, and her puddings come with bucketloads of that.

Ginger is not to everyone's liking, but this pudding could convert anybody – it's a great example of a spicy dish that goes perfectly with double cream or custard, or even with Greek yoghurt, my personal preference.

Bradford

SPOTTED DICK

Puddings are what the English do better than anyone else and this is one of Porters favourites.

225g/8oz self-raising (self-rising) flour
pinch of salt
110g/4oz/½ cup shredded suet (shortening)
*75g/3oz/3 tablespoons golden caster (milled golden
    cane) sugar*
*225g/8oz/1¼ cups sultanas (white raisins), soaked in
    brandy*
150ml/5fl oz/generous ½ cup cold water

Grease a 1.2-litre/2-pint/5-cup pudding basin. Sieve together the flour and salt, then add the suet, sugar and dried fruit. Add enough cold water to make a firm dough, then put the dough into the basin, cover securely and steam for 2 hours. Turn the pudding out on to a hot dish and serve with custard.

'Dick' seems to have been a general term for pudding in the nineteenth century. Queen Victoria had a sweet tooth and sweets and puddings were among her favourite dishes. Her consort, the German Prince Albert, brought about a revival of suet and steamed puddings.

JAM ROLY POLY

A hearty, comforting pudding that needs a well-flavoured dark jam to contrast with the pale pastry. The addition of lemon zest gives a lift to the rather bland suet pastry.

175g/6oz self-raising (self-rising) flour
grated zest of 1 small lemon
pinch of salt
75g/3oz/6 tablespoons shredded suet (shortening)
150ml/5fl oz/generous ½ cup cold water
225g/8oz/¾ cup strawberry, raspberry or
   blackcurrant jam (preserves)

Preheat the oven to 220°C/425°F/gas mark 7. Combine the flour, lemon zest, salt and suet in a mixing bowl and mix to a firm dough with the water. Roll out on a floured surface into a rectangle 20 × 30cm/8 × 12in. Spread with a thick layer of jam, roll up firmly and place on a greased baking tray. Bake for 30–40 minutes until golden brown.

In some regions this pudding was called 'Suety Jack' and could be boiled or baked. Originally it would have been boiled in a cloth in a pan hung over the fire. Sweet suet puddings such as this were very popular with families, as they were filling and economical to make.

SUSSEX POND PUDDING

This pudding is seldom seen nowadays, which is a pity because it's well worth the little trouble it takes to make. The lemon becomes very soft during cooking and blends into the butter and sugar to produce a rich lemon-flavoured sauce which oozes out when the pudding is cut open – hence the name.

225g/8oz self-raising (self-rising) flour
110g/4oz/4 tablespoons shredded suet (shortening)
150ml/5fl oz/generous ½ cup milk and water, mixed
110g/4oz/1 stick butter, diced
110g/4oz/¾ cup light muscovado (light brown muscovado) sugar
50g/2oz/4 tablespoons currants (optional)
1 large lemon

Combine the flour and suet in a mixing bowl and add the liquid. Mix to a soft dough and roll out on a floured surface into a large circle. Reserve a quarter of the circle of dough for the lid. Line a well-buttered 1.5-litre/2½-pint/6½-cup pudding basin with the pastry. Put half the butter and half the sugar into the pastry-lined basin and scatter in the currants, if using. Prick the lemon all over with a skewer and place whole on top of the butter and sugar. Cover with the rest of the butter and sugar. Lay the reserved pastry over the filling and press the edges together to seal completely. Cover with greaseproof paper with a pleat folded in the middle to allow the pudding to rise and cover this with pleated foil. Tie securely and put the basin into a large pan of boiling water so that the water comes halfway up the sides of the basin. Cover the pan and boil for 3½ hours, replenishing with boiling water as needed. Ease the sides of the pudding away from the basin with a palette knife. Turn out the pudding very carefully into a deep dish. Serve immediately, making sure that everyone gets a piece of lemon.

REAL BAKEWELL PUDDING

There are no almonds in this recipe but if you want an almond flavour add a few drops of real almond extract to the topping mixture.

225g/8oz shortcrust (pie) or puff pastry
good-quality strawberry or raspberry jam (preserves)
110g/4oz/1 stick butter
110g/4oz/½ cup golden caster (milled golden cane)
  sugar
4 egg yolks
3 egg whites

Preheat the oven to 200°C/400°F/gas mark 6. Roll out the pastry and line a 20cm/8in pie dish or flan tin (if you want to be really authentic, the baking dish should be oval with sloping sides). Spread the jam (preserves) in a thick layer over the base of the pastry. Melt the butter and pour it over the sugar and eggs, beating well. Pour the mixture over the jam and bake for 20–30 minutes until golden brown. Eat while still hot and fresh.

THE ORIGINS OF
BAKEWELL PUDDING

The town of Bakewell in Derbyshire is well known for its famous pudding, often incorrectly called Bakewell tart. Legend has it that the pudding was created by accident in the nineteenth century when the cook at the Rutland Arms in the town was making a jam tart and absent-mindedly poured the egg mixture intended for the pastry on top of the jam instead. However, a much more likely explanation is that Bakewell pudding was a variation of the popular 'transparent' puddings of the eighteenth century, in which a layer of fruit or jam was covered with a mixture of sugar, butter and eggs before baking. These puddings only occasionally had a pastry case and were more usually baked in a dish without the pastry. The famous cookery writer Eliza Acton recorded the first known recipe for Bakewell pudding in 1845 in *Modern Cookery for Private Families*, and wrote that it was 'served on all holiday occasions', although there was no mention of pastry. Mrs Beeton's recipe appeared with a puff pastry case in her *Book of Household Management* of 1861.

The jam can be replaced with stewed, candied or dried fruits, and the dried fruits can be soaked in wine or cider if you wish. In the summer months, use fresh raspberries sprinkled with golden caster (milled golden cane) sugar over the pastry base instead of jam. Authentic Bakewell pudding is deliciously rich and light. Nowadays its characteristic flavour is almonds, although these weren't used in the original dish. The mass-produced, commercial version of Derbyshire's famous pudding is Bakewell tart, which is a twentieth-century invention. Sadly, this is often a travesty of the original dish – made with cheap jam, synthetic almond flavouring and a covering of over-sweet icing. Some versions even include lurid, sticky glacé cherries. Ghastly!

NUTTY RHUBARB, ORANGE AND GINGER CRUMBLE

900g/2lb rhubarb* cut into 2.5cm/1in pieces
3 tablespoons light muscovado (light brown
*   muscovado) sugar*
2 teaspoons ground ginger
½ teaspoon ground cinnamon
75g/3oz/¾ cup plain (all-purpose) flour
pinch of salt
75g/3oz/¾ stick butter
3 tablespoons golden granulated (milled golden cane)
*   sugar*
75g/3oz/½ cup walnuts or hazelnuts, finely chopped
grated zest of 1 orange

Preheat the oven to 200°C/400°F/gas mark 6. Combine the rhubarb with the light muscovado (light brown muscovado) sugar until well coated and place in a buttered ovenproof dish. Sift the spices, flour and salt into a mixing bowl and rub in the butter until the mixture resembles bread-crumbs. Stir in the golden caster (milled golden cane) sugar, nuts and orange zest, and spoon evenly over the rhubarb. Cook for about 35 minutes until the crumble is golden and the filling is bubbling. Serve with custard, cream or ice cream.

* The leaves of the rhubarb plant contain oxalic acid and are highly poisonous, so they must be discarded. The leaves were once used as an insecticide, after shredding and mixing with water, to spray over plants and bushes.

Originally a native of Siberia, rhubarb seed was introduced into England from southern Siberia in the sixteenth century. It was initially grown in England as a medicinal plant in physic gardens, the roots being used as a purgative.

In the early seventeenth century rhubarb began to be cultivated as an ornamental plant in English gardens, where it flourished in the damp cold winter soil right through to the end of the often chilly summer. In the late eighteenth century someone discovered that the thick fleshy stems were edible and the stalks began to be used in pies and desserts for the first time. Mrs Beeton wrote in her *Book of Household Management* of 1861 that rhubarb 'was comparatively little known till within the last twenty or thirty years'.

APPLE FLORENTINE

Apple pies have always been an English favourite. This one is a little different in that sweetened spiced beer is poured into the cooked pie under the pastry case.

4 large cooking (green) apples
2 tablespoons golden granulated (milled golden cane) sugar
finely grated rind 1 lemon
225g/8oz shortcrust (pie) pastry
600ml/1 pint/2½ cups beer
pinch of grated nutmeg
pinch of ground cinnamon
pinch of ground cloves
1 tablespoon golden granulated (milled golden cane) sugar

Preheat the oven to 180°C/350°F/gas mark 4. Core the apples and leave them whole and unpeeled. Place in a deep pie dish and sprinkle with the sugar and lemon rind. Roll out the pastry and use to cover the apples. Bake for 30 minutes. Meanwhile, heat the beer, spices and sugar, but do not allow to boil. When the pie is ready, carefully lift off the pastry and pour the mixture over the apples. Cut the pastry into the required number of portions and place on top of the apples. Serve at once.

A FLORENDINE OF ORANGES AND APPLES

Apples and oranges make a delicious combination in this tart. The original recipe is given in Hannah Glasse's *The Art of Cookery made Plain and Easy*: 'Lay a puff paste all over the dish, spread marmalade over the bottom. Boil pippins, pared, quartered and cored, in a little water and sugar and slice two of the oranges and mix with the pippins in the dish; sprinkle with orange juice. Bake it in a slow oven for 30–40 minutes with a crust as above; or just bake the crust and lay in the ingredients.' What follows is a modern interpretation.

4 cooking (green) apples
3 tablespoons golden caster (milled golden cane)
*   sugar*
225g/8oz puff pastry
110g/4oz/¾ cup Seville orange marmalade
2 oranges, peeled and sliced
4 tablespoons orange juice

Preheat the oven to 180°C/350°F/gas mark 4. Peel, core and quarter the apples and poach them in a little water with the sugar until they are soft and tender but still retain their shape. Roll out the pastry and line a 20cm/8in flan dish. Spread the marmalade over the base. Arrange the apple quarters and sliced oranges in the pastry case and sprinkle with orange juice. Bake for 30–40 minutes. Serve warm.

Use a good-quality, well-flavoured marmalade, not the sweet 'jelly' type. Vary the flavour by using ginger or lemon marmalade.

THE FIRST MRS BEETON?

Hannah Glasse wrote the first best-selling cookery book, *The Art of Cookery made Plain and Easy – Which far exceeds any Thing of the Kind yet published – by a Lady*. Published in 1747, it remained phenomenally popular for the next 100 years. In fact it was so popular that a rumour was put about that it must have been written by a man! Although it was published anonymously at first, later editions, published after her death, have her signature in facsimile at the top of the text.

Mrs Glasse was a remarkable woman. Although little is known about her, it's believed that she married a lawyer when very young, had eight children and was also dressmaker to the Princess of Wales. *The Art of Cookery* was clearly written, easy to follow and intended for use by servants. Mrs Glasse declared, 'My intention is to instruct the lower sort . . . every servant who can read will be capable of making a tolerable good cook.' The recipes were more precise in measurements and method than in previous cookery books and were easier to understand. Her book also reflected the new standards of hygiene of the time and included instructions on how to clean cooking utensils and kitchen equipment. Until the eighteenth century, cookery books had been written by men for use by chefs in the wealthy and aristocratic great houses of the day. The rest of the population – in other words, the majority – had to rely on recipes handed down by word of mouth.

Mrs Glasse lived in the great days of English food (she had no time for fancy foreign food and was particularly critical of French chefs) and her deservedly popular book offers us a fascinating insight into the recipes and cooking styles of the eighteenth century. There are many wonderful old recipes worth reviving today. The first edition of *The Art of Cookery* is now very scarce and expensive.

Mrs Glasse also wrote two more successful books in 1760 – *The Compleat Confectioner* and *The Servant's Directory & Housekeeper's Companion!*

TREACLE TART

Commercially produced treacle tarts tend to be both overpoweringly sweet and claggy. This substitutes black treacle for some of the golden syrup and the flavour is sharpened with lemon zest and juice and a dash of cinnamon.

225g/8oz shortcrust (pie) pastry
2 tablespoons black treacle (molasses)
175g/6oz/½ cup golden (corn) syrup
75g/3oz/1½ cups fresh breadcrumbs
grated zest and juice of 1 lemon
½ teaspoon ground cinnamon

Preheat the oven to 190°C/375°F/gas mark 5. Roll out two-thirds of the pastry and line a 23cm/9in loose-based flan tin about 3cm/1¼in deep. Combine the remaining ingredients and mix well, then spoon into the pastry case, spreading the mixture evenly. Roll out the rest of the pastry and cut strips about 5mm/¼in wide, then twist the strips. Lay them on top of the tart in a lattice and bake for 20–30 minutes until the pastry is golden. Serve hot or cold.

Treacle (molasses), a by-product of sugar refining, was first imported into England from Genoa and Flanders in the fifteenth century. The sticky black viscous syrup was later sold by the newly established London sugar refineries as London Treacle. It replaced honey in gingerbread, being included in lavish amounts in gingerbread made for Charles II. By the late eighteenth century treacle was much used in the north of England. Golden syrup, also a by-product of sugar refining, was created at that time. In northern England, where there is a strong tradition of home baking, many open tarts were decorated with strips of pastry in traditional designs. Treacle tarts are always decorated with a pastry lattice.

WHITE LADIES PUDDING

Here the traditional recipe has been adapted to include coconut milk, which first became popular in the nineteenth century.

110g/4oz/1½ cups desiccated (dried and shredded) coconut
6 thin slices good-quality white bread, crusts removed and thickly buttered
600ml/1 pint/2½ cups milk
300ml/10fl oz/1¼ cups coconut milk
few drops vanilla essence (extract)
pinch of salt
4 eggs
75g/3oz/3 tablespoons golden granulated (milled golden cane) sugar

Preheat the oven to 180°C/350°F/gas mark 4. Scatter half the coconut over the base of a buttered 1.2-litre/2-pint/5-cup pie dish. Cut the buttered bread into triangles and arrange in the pie dish. Sprinkle with the remaining coconut. Heat the milk and coconut milk until warm, then add a few drops of vanilla essence (extract) and the salt. Beat in the eggs and sugar and pour over the bread. Leave to soak for 30 minutes, then place the pie dish in a roasting tin (pan) and pour in enough hot water to come halfway up the sides of the dish. Bake for 30–40 minutes or until set.

The ruins of White Ladies Priory are actually on our land, just down from Boscobel, where Charles II climbed the oak tree. A few miles away is Black Ladies, a magnificent sixteenth-century building near the Staffordshire town of Brewood, which is still lived in. Naturally the names of the orders of nuns excite more interest than they should!

Bradford

The Dominican nuns of Worcestershire created this tasty bread pudding, which became known as White Ladies Pudding due to the familiar white habits of the order. The recipe is well worth reviving and is an unusual variation on the more usual fruited bread and butter pudding.

The English word coconut, first mentioned in print in 1555, comes from the Spanish and Portuguese word '*coco*', which means monkey face. The Spanish and Portuguese explorers thought that the three round indented markings or 'eyes' found at the base of the coconut resembled a grinning monkey's face. Sir Francis Drake wrote, 'Amongst other things we found here a kind of fruit called Cocos, which because it is not commonly knowen with us in England, I thought good to make some description of it.' Early spellings of coconut were cocoanut and coker-nut.

LUXURY BREAD AND BUTTER PUDDING

A delightfully rich and creamy variation on an old favourite and an excellent way of using up stale fruit loaf or bread.

110g/4oz slightly stale fruit loaf
50g/2oz/½ stick butter
4 tablespoons bitter orange or ginger marmalade
300ml/10fl oz/1¼ cups single (light) cream
1 teaspoon vanilla essence (extract)
3 egg yolks
50g/2oz/¼ cup golden caster (milled golden cane) sugar

Preheat the oven to 150°C/300°F/gas mark 2. Slice the bread and spread first with the butter, then with 2 tablespoons marmalade. Slice diagonally in half and arrange in a buttered baking dish, spread side down. Heat the cream to boiling point, then remove from the heat and stir in the vanilla essence (extract). Whisk the egg yolks with the sugar and pour on the cream, whisking all the time. Strain over the bread and leave to soak for 2 hours. Place the dish in a roasting tin (pan) and pour in enough hot water to come halfway up the sides of the dish. Bake for 40–45 minutes until the top is golden brown and the pudding is set but still has a slight wobble. Remove from oven and brush with the remaining warmed marmalade. Serve with custard or cream.

If we ever want to really impress visitors from abroad, or friends when we are out in Spain, a special bread and butter pudding is the best way. To my eternal disappointment, it is guaranteed to always get finished off, as I love it warmed up again the next day.

The marvellous thing about bread and butter pudding is that you can vary what goes into it to achieve the desired result: use more cream to beef it up or a little milk instead to make it less rich, add chocolate or rum, soak the sultanas in amaretto, use brioche or fruit loaf – the permutations are endless. The most important thing to remember, though, is to get the proportions of bread to egg custard right, as you don't want it to be stodgy.

Bradford

Bread puddings – a simple mixture of boiled bread and other ingredients to hand – were among the earliest puddings. Bread has always been filling and inexpensive. Bowls of bread and warm milk were staple fare for children and invalids. Many recipes based on these simple ingredients were developed, incorporating over time sugar, dried fruits and spices as they became cheaper and more widely available. Impoverished students at Oxford and Cambridge in the past were fed heavy bread pudding enlivened with spices and dried fruits to satisfy their appetites.

POOR KNIGHTS OF WINDSOR

Americans know this as 'French Toast', but the wine or cream and spices here elevate it to the luxury class. This is delicious served with fresh raspberries.

3–4 tablespoons white wine or single (light) cream

2–3 tablespoons golden granulated (milled golden cane) sugar, plus extra for sprinkling

8 slices of good-quality stale white bread, 2.5cm/1in thick

2 egg yolks, beaten

110g/4oz/1 stick butter

ground cinnamon or freshly grated nutmeg

Put the wine and sugar into a dish and add the bread slices, turning them over once. Remove each slice carefully and dip it into the beaten egg yolk. Heat the butter in a frying pan until foaming and fry the slices until crisp and golden. Drain and place on a hot dish and sprinkle with sugar and spice.

AN ANCIENT BREAD PUDDING

This delightfully named pudding dates from around the thirteenth century. It was also known as 'Pampurdy', which is a corruption of the French *pain perdue*, which means 'lost or smothered bread'. Slices of the finest-quality white bread were dipped into beaten egg yolks before being fried in clarified butter and sprinkled with sugar and perhaps rose water and spices. In England the dish is called Poor Knights of Windsor, although the reasons for this association are not known. The Poor Knights, established by Edward III, were a community of 26 impoverished military veterans. They were given food and lodging from the new college of St George at Windsor, founded by Edward III, in return for praying for the king and the knights of the order. In accordance with the wishes of her father, Henry VIII, Elizabeth I reduced the number of Poor Knights to thirteen. In 1834 they were renamed Military Knights.

In the early seventeenth century it became customary to add cream to the spiced yolks and the dish was known variously as Cream Toast, Pan Perdy or Poor Knights of Windsor. Other variations of the recipe that have appeared over the years include soaking the bread slices in wine and sugar before dipping in the egg yolk, as here.

TIPSY SUMMER PUDDING

A simple but sensational pudding that epitomises summer. Use the freshest, ripe juicy berries you can find and excellent white bread.

6–8 slices good-quality white bread, crusts removed
675g/1½lb/4 cups summer berries, e.g. strawberries,
*   blackcurrants, raspberries, etc.*
110g/4oz/½ cup golden caster (milled golden cane)
*   sugar*
2 tablespoons red wine or fruit liqueur, e.g. cassis,
*   framboise, etc.*

Cut the bread into 1cm/½in slices and use some to cover the base of a 900ml/1½-pint/4-cup pudding basin. Line the sides of the basin with more bread, making sure there are no gaps. Put the fruit into a pan with the sugar and wine and bring to simmering point. Simmer gently for 2–3 minutes, until the sugar has dissolved and the juices run from the fruit. Remove from the heat. Spoon the fruit and juice into the bread-lined basin, reserving some juice for later. Cover the top with bread. Stand the basin on a deep plate (to catch any overflowing juices) and put a plate large enough to fit inside the bowl on top of the pudding. Place a heavy weight on top of the plate (cans of food or bags of sugar are ideal) and chill overnight. Run a knife around the edge of the pudding and invert a serving plate on top of the pudding. Turn out and carefully remove the basin. Spoon the reserved juices over any parts of the bread that have not been soaked with juice. Serve with whipped cream.

It's possible that the recipe for this delightful summery dessert is very old, as the ingredients were easy to obtain and the pudding is simple to make. It was known as hydropathic pudding in the eighteenth century, when it was regarded as the ideal sweet for invalids, who were not allowed the rich pastry desserts in vogue at the time.

BAKED QUINCE

You may be lucky enough to have a quince tree in your garden, but if not quinces can be found in ethnic food stores and also in some large supermarkets in the autumn (fall). Don't store quinces near other fruits as their penetrating perfume will be absorbed by them.

6 quinces
lemon juice
25g/1oz/¼ stick butter
500ml-1 litre/1-1½ pints/3–4 cups water
220ml/8fl oz/1 cup red or white wine
50ml/2fl oz/⅓ cup honey
110g/4oz/½ cup golden caster (milled golden cane)
    sugar
1 cinnamon stick, broken in half
1 whole clove

Preheat the oven to 200°C/400°F/gas mark 6. Wash and scrub the quinces well to remove the downy covering, then peel, core and quarter them with a sharp knife. Sprinkle with lemon juice to avoid discoloration. Place the quinces in a buttered ovenproof dish that will hold them snugly. Combine the remaining ingredients and pour over the fruit. Lightly cover with foil and bake for 20 minutes. Remove the foil covering and bake for another 20 minutes or until the fruit is tender. Leave to cool in the dish. Serve warm with cream or ice cream.

Baked quince was the favourite pudding of Sir Isaac Newton. This exquisitely perfumed fruit, which is inedible when raw but delectable when cooked, has inexplicably fallen out of favour in England, although in the Middle Ages and up until the nineteenth century it was baked and eaten as a dessert with cream and was also made into marmalade and jellies. Greenish gold in colour, covered with patches of greyish down (which must be removed before cooking), quinces contain lots of pips. Closely related to the apple, they are one of the best flavourings for apple dishes and also go well with pears.

BAKED APPLES

In this recipe the sugar and cider or apple juice combine to form a delicious syrup as the apples are cooking.

6 large apples
110g/4oz/1 stick butter
110g/4oz/¾ cup sultanas (golden raisins)
110g/4oz/1 scant cup walnuts, chopped
110g/4oz/¾ cup dark muscovado (dark brown
  molasses) sugar
1 teaspoon ground cinnamon (optional)
225ml/7fl oz/1 scant cup cider or apple juice

Preheat the oven to 180°C/350°F/gas mark 4. Butter 6 squares of foil each large enough to wrap an apple. Peel and core the apples and place them on their pieces of foil. Cream two-thirds of the butter until soft and stir in the sultanas and walnuts. Spoon the mixture into the centre of each apple. Dot with the remaining butter and sprinkle with sugar and cinnamon, if using. Pour the cider or apple juice carefully over and around the apples. Loosely wrap the foil around each apple to form a parcel and seal the edges well. Bake for about 25–30 minutes until the apples are soft.

Just one of my absolute favourites, but then I am a sucker for anything with fruit in it. This is a wonderfully simple dish, with additions that lift it out of the ordinary and into a special class of its own. The joy comes from spooning the mixture of juices, walnuts and sultanas over the warm apple.

Try experimenting with different ingredients. Apples are great baked with a little quantity of marmalade in the middle, for instance. In fact, almost anything that goes with apples can be used, like treacle and dried apricots. Don't be scared to try.

Bradford

> Apples are one of England's best-loved fruits. In the thirteenth century they were grown by the monks of Westminster in their huge garden – now Covent Garden – and later at Hampton Court in King Henry VIII's orchards.

APPLE AND MINT WHIP

A light and luscious Porters dessert.

450g/1lb cooking (green) apples
50g/2oz/¼ cup golden caster (milled golden cane)
*   sugar*
1 tablespoon water
600ml/1 pint/2½ cups double (heavy) cream
1 tablespoon chopped mint leaves
golden icing (confectioners') sugar and mint leaves to
*   garnish*

Peel, core and slice the apples. Place the apples, sugar and water in a medium-sized pan and cook over a moderate heat for 20 minutes, stirring occasionally. Allow the mixture to cool slightly, check the sweetness, adding a little icing (confectioners') sugar if necessary, and blend in a food processor. Chill for 30 minutes. Whisk the cream to soft peaks. Gently fold in the apple purée and chopped mint leaves. Transfer to serving dishes (martini glasses would be ideal) and chill for at least 30 minutes. Serve garnished with mint leaves and sprinkled with icing sugar.

BURNT TRINITY COFFEE CREAMS

Everyone loves this creamy coffee dessert with its golden toffee topping. The topping should be thin, so that it cracks easily when tapped with a spoon.

½ vanilla pod (bean)
150ml/5fl oz/generous ½ cup milk
300ml/10fl oz/1¼ cups single (light) cream
50ml/2fl oz/¼ cup coffee essence or cold strong coffee
4 eggs
75g/3oz/3 tablespoons golden granulated (milled
*   golden cane) sugar*

for the topping
1½ tablespoons golden caster (milled golden cane)
*   sugar*
1½ tablespoons golden granulated (milled golden
*   cane) sugar*

Preheat the oven to 100°C/212°F/gas mark ½. Split the half vanilla pod (bean) and place in the cream. Allow to infuse for as long as possible, then strain the cream into a bowl. Add all the other ingredients and whisk until combined. Pour into 4 ovenproof ramekins and place these in a roasting tin. Pour in enough hot water to come halfway up the sides of the ramekins. Cook for about 1 hour or until firm. Allow to cool. Just before serving, sprinkle the top with an even mix of golden caster and golden granulated (milled golden cane) sugar. Place under a very hot grill or use a blow torch to melt the sugar, forming a caramelised crust. Serve immediately.

Sadly, as an undergraduate at Trinity College in the late 1960s, this never seemed to be served in the students' dining hall; presumably it was reserved for the High Table, where the dons sat.

Having read about the history of the dish, I was longing to sample the 'real thing', but then maybe the chefs in the kitchens there were not capable enough. Certainly the rest of the food was nothing to get excited about.

Bradford

This luscious dish was said to have first been made at Trinity College, Cambridge, in the nineteenth century. The story goes that an undergraduate knew the recipe from a country house in Aberdeenshire and offered it to the college kitchens in the 1860s. The offer was refused, but when the undergraduate became a Fellow the recipe was accepted and quickly became popular at the May Week festivities. However, this charming story is discounted by the fact that a recipe for burnt cream appeared as early as 1769 in Mrs Raffald's book *The Experienced English Housekeeper*. Earlier eighteenth-century recipes for a similarly rich baked egg cream also appeared in handwritten cookery books, flavoured with either orange-flower water or wine, although these didn't have the crisp caramel topping.

SYLLABUB

220ml/8fl oz/½ cup sweet white wine
large pinch grated nutmeg
peel of 1 lemon
2 tablespoons brandy
2 tablespoons golden caster (milled golden
  cane) sugar
220ml/8fl oz/1 cup double (heavy) cream

Place the wine, nutmeg, lemon peel and brandy in a bowl, cover and leave overnight. The next day strain the mixture into a bowl and add the sugar, stirring until dissolved. Still stirring, slowly pour in the cream. Whisk the mixture until it holds its shape, but don't over-beat or the cream will curdle. Spoon into 4 dishes and chill for 2–3 hours. Serve with small crisp biscuits (cookies).

THE STORY OF
SYLLABUB

Rich and creamy alcoholic syllabub has a long history dating back to Tudor times. The name derives from Sill, the area in France from which *sille* wine came, and *bub*, which was Elizabethan slang for a bubbling drink. Originally, syllabub was a festive drink based on wine, cider or beer, mixed with sweetened milk and well flavoured with spices. Charles II was reputedly so fond of it that he ordered a herd of cows to be kept in St James's Park so that a supply of milk would always be on hand to make his syllabub.

In the late seventeenth century a special wooden cow was available from which the milk and cream could be squirted from a height into a bowl. Like a live cow, this wooden one also produced a beverage with a frothy top and a clear liquid underneath. The creamy froth was eaten with a spoon, then the liquid was drunk. Special serving vessels with spouts enabled the imbiber to drink the liquid beneath the creamy curd separately. A handheld whisk replaced the wooden cow in Georgian times. Orange and lemon juice was also used during this period to make non-alcoholic confections known as fruit syllabubs.

As time passed, cream replaced milk, giving the syllabub a thicker top on its liquid base. This type of drink was known as a whipped syllabub. In 1665, in the second edition of *The Accomplisht Cook*, Robert May gave a recipe for a syllabub made with cider, sugar, nutmeg, and cream. The cream was added a few spoonfuls at a time, then the mixture was beaten hard and left to stand for several hours to separate. Special sets consisting of a large deep bowl, a ladle and tall, narrow glasses were sold for the making and serving of syllabub.

A new development was the so-called everlasting syllabub. A favourite dessert in eighteenth-century England, this variation got its name because it could be left to stand for a long time without separating, thanks to the greater proportion of cream used. To make everlasting syllabub, cream was mixed with sweetened wine, brandy or sherry. Lemon or orange juice was added, as were twists of lemon peel and sprigs of rosemary for decoration. Several different types of syllabub were prepared throughout the eighteenth century. Mrs Copley's *The Housekeeper's Guide* of 1834 mentions some regional variations:

London syllabub – made with port or white wine
Hampshire syllabub – made with strong beer and brandy
Punch syllabub – made with lemon juice, rum and brandy

DEVONSHIRE JUNKET

An earlier and altogether more sophisticated version of what became a nursery pudding in the early twentieth century, when artificially coloured and flavoured junket tablets and powders appeared on the market. Once the luxury dish had turned into nursery fare, junket fell from favour.

600ml/1 pint/2½ cups milk
25g/1oz/1 tablespoon golden granulated (milled
    golden cane) sugar
2 tablespoons brandy
1 teaspoon liquid rennet
clotted cream and freshly grated nutmeg to finish
    (optional)

Heat the milk in a pan to blood heat (36.6°–37.7°C/98°–100°F) – that is, hot but bearable to the touch. Add the sugar and brandy and stir well. Pour into a large serving bowl and gently stir in the rennet. Leave to stand undisturbed for at least an hour until set. Spread with clotted cream and sprinkle with nutmeg if liked.

A   BRIEF   HISTORY   OF
JUNKET

Curdled milk was used to make junket, a dish of sweetened curds. Old cookery books sometimes listed curds and whey (as eaten by Miss Muffet of the nursery rhyme) as junkets. The name comes from the Old Norman French *jonquet*, a small basket made of *jonques* or rushes, which was used to drain the curds. English junket evolved from an Old French dish made of renneted cream in which the curds were broken up and drained of whey, then flavoured with sugar and spices. Later it was customary to add rose water and sugar and eat it as a sweet after a meal.

The dish of sweetened creamy curds, frequently flavoured with spices, featured so often at fairs held on religious holidays that the holidays themselves became known as 'junketing days'.

English potteries in the seventeenth and eighteenth centuries produced elegant, wide, deep junket bowls that held as much as 4 litres/7 pints/17½ cups. Junket remained popular until the eighteenth century, when the much easier and far less time-consuming unrenneted cream-based syllabubs and fools came into vogue. However, as late as the nineteenth century junket was still being sold in glasses or mugs from London street stalls.

TEA CREAM

25g/1oz green tea
3 tablespoons golden caster (milled golden cane) sugar
¼ teaspoon coriander seeds, crushed
½ cinnamon stick
finely pared rind of 1 lemon
300ml/10fl oz/1¼ cups single (light) cream
300ml/10fl oz/1¼ cups double (heavy) cream
5 gelatine leaves
4 tablespoons cold water

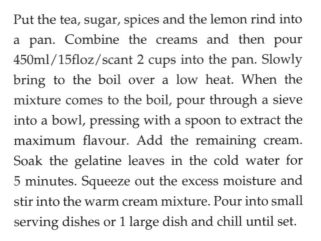

Put the tea, sugar, spices and the lemon rind into a pan. Combine the creams and then pour 450ml/15floz/scant 2 cups into the pan. Slowly bring to the boil over a low heat. When the mixture comes to the boil, pour through a sieve into a bowl, pressing with a spoon to extract the maximum flavour. Add the remaining cream. Soak the gelatine leaves in the cold water for 5 minutes. Squeeze out the excess moisture and stir into the warm cream mixture. Pour into small serving dishes or 1 large dish and chill until set.

> An early-eighteenth-century dessert that uses green or gunpowder tea – an unfermented tea with a strong flavour. Early recipes included the chopped melted gizzards of chickens, which were later replaced by rennet. It became a very fashionable dessert but was later eclipsed by coffee cream.

STRAWBERRY AND ROSE-WATER MOUSSE

There's nothing to beat English strawberries – summer and Wimbledon would be unimaginable without this fragrant soft fruit. Here is an elegant light dessert perfect for a warm summer's evening.

450g/1lb/2½ cups
strawberries, hulled, a few reserved for decoration
3 tablespoons cold water
15g/½oz powdered gelatine
110g/4oz/½ cup golden caster (milled golden cane)
*   sugar*
juice of 1 lemon
1 tablespoon rose water
150ml/5fl oz/generous ½ cup double (heavy) cream
2 egg whites

Reserve a few strawberries for decoration and push the rest through a sieve to make a purée. Put half the purée into a pan. Put the water into a cup and sprinkle over the gelatine. Leave to stand for 5 minutes. Add the sugar, lemon juice and soaked gelatine to the purée in the pan and heat gently until the sugar has dissolved. Do not allow to boil as this will destroy the setting properties of the gelatine. Remove from the heat and stir in the remaining purée. Add the rose water. Leave to stand for 10–15 minutes until the mixture begins to set. Whisk the cream until thick but not stiff. Whisk the egg whites until stiff. Gently fold the cream into the strawberry mixture, followed by the egg whites. Divide between 6 serving glasses and chill until firm. Decorate with slices of the reserved strawberries.

IN CELEBRATION OF STRAWBERRIES

Wild strawberries have been enjoyed for thousands of years, but it wasn't until around 1300 that the fruit, known first as the 'straeberie' was cultivated in gardens. How the name originated is something of a mystery, but it could be because the berries used to be threaded on straws of grass to make it easier to carry them to market, or because straw was placed around the fruiting plants to protect them from frost. Possibly the name comes from the Saxon *streoberie* or *streawberige*, so called perhaps because the plant's runners stray away in all directions. It could also be a corruption of 'strewberry', since the berries are strewn among the leaves of the plant.

In the Middle Ages the berries symbolised perfection and purity and in art the Virgin Mary was often depicted with strawberries. Stonemasons of the time carved strawberry designs on the altars and stone pillars of churches and cathedrals. The highly prized strawberry was also served at important banquets and feasts to ensure peace and prosperity.

The last word must go to a seventeenth-century English writer, Dr William Butler, who opined, 'Doubtless God could have made a better berry, but doubtless God never did.'

REAL TRIFLE

A proper trifle is a sumptuous concoction of cake, creamy custard, alcohol and fresh cream, with no layer of jelly (jello) in between – and definitely no garishly coloured 'hundred and thousands' scattered over the top.

12 sponge fingers
raspberry jam (preserves)
110g/4oz ratafia biscuits
75ml/3fl oz/3 tablespoons sweet sherry
3 tablespoons orange or other fruit liqueur (optional)
110g/4oz/1 cup raspberries
600ml/1 pint/2½ cups thick custard
450ml/15fl oz/2 cups double (heavy) cream
25g/1oz golden icing (confectioners') sugar
crystallised rose petals, toasted flaked almonds and
*   raspberries to decorate*

Spread the sponge fingers liberally with the jam, then break them up and place in a glass or china serving dish with the crumbled ratafias. Mix the sherry with the liqueur, if using, and pour over the sponge fingers and ratafias, mixing very gently and leave until the liquid is absorbed.

Scatter over the raspberries, then spoon the custard on top. Whip the cream and icing (confectioners') sugar until soft peaks form and spread on top of the custard. Decorate with crystallised rose petals, toasted flaked almonds and raspberries just before serving.

You can vary this trifle by using chocolate sponge cake instead of sponge fingers; chocolate or coffee liqueur and another type of fruit, e.g. mandarin oranges. Decorate with grated chocolate.

The first known recipe for 'A Trifle' was in Thomas Dawson's the *Good Housewife's Jewell* of 1596. It was a mixture of thick cream, sugar, ginger and rose water, heated together and served lukewarm. By the eighteenth century trifle had acquired a cake base, covered with thick custard and was topped with syllabub and sprinkled with comfits (sugar-coated spices – caraway seeds, for example).

BROWN BREAD ICE CREAM

The breadcrumbs, which must be wholemeal (whole wheat), and sugar are caramelised into delicious sweet crunchy pieces.

110g/4oz/2 cups wholemeal (whole wheat)
    breadcrumbs
110g/4oz/½ cup demerara sugar
600ml/1 pint/2½ cups double (heavy) cream
2 tablespoons rum or 1 teaspoon vanilla essence
    (extract)

Preheat the oven to 190°C/375°F/gas mark 5. Mix together the breadcrumbs and sugar and spread out on a greased baking tray. Place in the oven for 20–30 minutes, stirring now and again with a fork. Leave to cool. Whisk the cream until soft peaks form and then gently fold in the rum or vanilla essence (extract) and cold caramelised crumbs. Spoon into a freezer-proof container, cover and place in the freezer until half frozen. Remove from the freezer and whisk vigorously to break down any ice crystals. Turn into a loaf tin lined with cling film (plastic wrap) and press down well. Cover and freeze until firm. Transfer the ice cream to the refrigerator about 30 minutes before serving.

I C E D
D E L I G H T S

The earliest reference to ice cream in England is in 1672 in 'the Institution, Laws and Ceremonies of the most Noble Order of the Garter' by Elias Ashmole (published by Nathanael Brooke, London, 1672), when it appeared in a list of foods served at the Feast of St George at Windsor as 'One Plate of Ice Cream', although this delicacy was served only at the king's table. The accounts of the lord steward's department of 1686 tell us that ice cream was purchased for King James II. Later, ice cream was served at the tables of the fashionable well-to-do in the early eighteenth century. The first published recipe in an English cookery book dates from 1718 and was given by Mrs Mary Eales, 'Confectioner to her late Majesty Queen Anne'. Brown bread ice cream was a nineteenth-century favourite and was also popular with the Edwardians.

EARL GREY ICE CREAM

It's always nice to serve something homemade that can't be bought in the shops and this unusual ice cream fits the bill.

*150m/5fl oz/generous ½ cup very strong Earl Grey
    tea (without milk)*
150ml/5fl oz/generous ½ cup milk
150ml/5fl oz/generous ½ cup single (light) cream
strip of lemon peel
3 egg yolks
*110g/4oz/½ cup golden caster (milled golden cane)
    sugar*
150ml/5fl oz/generous ½ cup whipping cream

Put the tea, milk and single (light) cream into a pan with the lemon peel and heat gently to simmering point. Remove from the heat. Whisk the egg yolks and sugar together until thick and pale, then whisk in the hot milk mixture. Discard the lemon peel and return the mixture to the pan. Cook over a very low heat until it thickens, but do not allow to boil or the mixture will curdle. Leave until cold, placing a piece of damp grease-proof (waxed) paper on the surface. Pour into a freezer-proof container, cover and freeze until half frozen. Turn into a bowl and whisk vigorously. Whip the cream until thick and fold into the mixture. Return to the container and freeze until firm. Place in the refrigerator 30 minutes before serving.

Earl Grey tea owes its delicate flavour to the addition of bergamot oil. The story goes that the recipe was given to the second Earl Grey in the nineteenth century by a Chinese mandarin whose life had been saved by a British diplomat. It imparts a tantalising taste to this ice cream.

AFTERNOON TEA

Tea was an important new and fashionable drink in seventeenth-century England and was imported in small quantities by the East India Company. Known for centuries in China, both as a drink and as a culinary ingredient – tea leaves were also made into cakes with rice and spices. Catherine, the wife of Charles II, encouraged tea drinking at court and the East India Company soon began importing china tea 'dishes', teapots and also sugar bowls.

The wives of the nobility quickly adopted the custom of serving tea to friends, and the cost added an extra cachet to their social standing. Tea was expensive and kept in locked caddies. Just a pinch of the costly leaves was infused in boiled water for 2–3 minutes. At first no milk was added, although tea was sweetened with sugar.

Social tea drinking was encouraged when Thomas Twining (of the now famous tea company) opened the first tea shop for ladies in 1717 in London. Fifteen years later, London's Vauxhall pleasure gardens were developed into a tea garden and its success led to the opening of more on the outskirts of London and in other towns.

By the 1740s, it was usual to add milk to one's cup of tea and to accompany it with buttered bread or toast. Tea was also drunk after dinner, and when the fashionable time for dinner advanced from around 3 p.m. to 6 or 7 p.m. a new meal, afternoon tea, was established to bridge the gap between a late breakfast and dinner.

Her Majesty the Queen's favourite afternoon tea usually includes Dundee cake, raspberry and strawberry jam (preserves) and a pot of Earl Grey tea.

SUGARED CURRANT CAKES

Sweet buttery little cakes, which are enriched with ground almonds.

250g/9oz/2¼ cups self-raising (self-rising) flour
¼ teaspoon ground mixed spice (pumpkin spice)
pinch of cinnamon
50g/2oz/4 tablespoons currants
50g/2oz/½ cup ground almonds
200g/7oz/scant cup golden granulated (milled golden
*   cane) sugar*
110g/4oz/1 stick butter, melted
1 egg, beaten
golden granulated (milled golden cane) sugar and
*   ground cinnamon for sprinkling*

Preheat the oven to 200°C/400°F/gas mark 6. Sift the flour and spices into a mixing bowl and stir in the currants, ground almonds and sugar. Add the melted butter and the egg, and mix to a soft dough. Roll out on a floured surface into a rectangle about 25 × 30cm/10 × 12in. Brush the dough with water and sprinkle with the extra sugar and cinnamon. Roll up like a Swiss roll and cut into slices about 2cm/¾in thick. Place these well apart on a greased baking tray and bake for 10–15 minutes until lightly browned. Cool on a wire rack.

Sugar was first mentioned in England in the Royal Rolls of 1205. The returning Crusaders had encountered it on their travels and knew it as 'honey cane'. It was enormously expensive, but as time passed it became less costly, though still only the wealthy could afford it.

Elizabethans loved sugar and none more so than Elizabeth I herself, who was very fond of sweet, sugary foods (especially currant cakes), as a result of which her teeth became quite black as she got older. In the later part of her reign the amounts of sugar in England increased greatly and sugar loaves were used as bribes and given as gifts. Sugar featured extensively in both savoury and sweet dishes for the wealthy. Sir John Harrington, the Queen's godson and favourite, would invent new sweetmeats to cheer her up when she was depressed.

BRIGHTON ROCK CAKES

Rose water imparts an intriguing flavour to these tempting little cakes.

75g/3oz/¾ stick butter
75g/3oz/3 tablespoons golden caster (milled golden cane) sugar
75g/3oz/generous ½ cup ground almonds
110g/4oz/¾ cup sultanas (golden raisins)
140g/5oz/generous cup plain (all-purpose) flour
2 eggs, beaten
1 teaspoon rose water (optional)
beaten egg to glaze

Preheat the oven to 220°C/425°F/gas mark 7. Beat the butter and sugar together until light and creamy. Add the ground almonds and sultanas (golden raisins), then stir in the flour, eggs and rose water. Mix to a stiff dough and place small mounds – you will get about 10 or 12 – on a greased baking tray. Glaze the buns with a little beaten egg and bake for 12–15 minutes. Cool on a wire rack.

ROSES IN COOKING

The fragile beauty and delightful fragrance of the rose has been prized for thousands of years. Roses were cultivated in the herb and kitchen gardens of monasteries and private houses. Medieval cooks used highly perfumed red rose petals to flavour sauces and fruit pies, and for many years, until fairly recently, roses remained an important culinary ingredient of savoury and sweet dishes, drinks and medicinal syrups. Every part of the plant – buds, hips and leaves, as well as the petals – could be used in recipes for such delicacies as rose honey, rose-scented vinegar, rose jams and jellies. Rose water, with its wonderful heady perfume, was distilled from damask rose petals.

Heavily scented rose petals were scattered over cherries before they were covered with pastry and baked in a pie. Crystallised petals, made by boiling them in a sugar or honey and water syrup, were used to decorate creamy sweets such as syllabubs and fruit tarts. Rose water was used to flavour sweetmeats, desserts and puddings; was sprinkled on fruit during the candying process; was mixed with sugar to make an icing for sweet pies; and was used as a binding agent for cake mixtures – it was more reliable than the doubtful water supply of the time. Rose water always featured whenever a recipe called for almonds to be 'pounded', as it prevented them from 'oiling'.

RICHMOND MAIDS OF HONOUR

There are lots of recipes for these little tarts. This version is an amalgamation of them all.

225g/8oz shortcrust (pie) or puff pastry
110g/4oz/¾ cup curd cheese
75g/3oz/¾ stick butter
1 egg
1 tablespoon rose water or brandy
75g/3oz/3 tablespoons golden caster (milled golden
    cane) sugar
50g/2oz/½ cup ground almonds
finely grated zest of 1 lemon

Preheat the oven to 200°C/400°F/gas mark 6. Roll out the pastry and line 10–12 deep tartlet or bun tins. Beat the cheese and butter together until smooth. Beat in the egg and rose water or brandy, followed by the sugar, almonds and lemon zest. Spoon into the pastry cases to half-fill them. Bake for 20–25 minutes until risen and golden. Remove from the oven and place on a wire rack to cool. The tarts will sink a little.

THE STORY OF MAIDS OF HONOUR

Legend has it that these delicious little cheesecakes were first made in the kitchens of Richmond Palace or Hampton Court and served to Henry VIII. One version of the story says that he named them after Anne Boleyn, who before she was queen was a maid of honour to his first wife, Catherine of Aragon. Another relates that the recipe was locked away in an iron box until it was rediscovered by Henry VIII, who presented it to Anne Boleyn. She is said to have made the tarts for Henry, who in turn named them after her. Yet another has it that Henry came across Anne and her maids of honour eating the cakes from a silver dish and, after tasting them, was so delighted that he named them after the maids of honour and the recipe was kept secret.

Ultimately, the recipe appeared in the second edition (1665) of Robert May's *The Accomplisht Cook*. Commercial production began in Hill Street, Richmond, in 1750 and 'the original shop of the Maids of Honour' survived there until 1957. In 1850 one Robert Newens, who had served his apprenticeship at the Hill Street bakery, opened a shop in King Street, Richmond, later moving to 3 George Street, where he continued making and selling the maids of honour. In 1887 Robert's son, Alfred, opened a new shop at 288–290 Kew

Road, Kew, where he also made maids of honour from the recipe passed on by his father. Alfred died in 1927, when the business was carried on by his son John and daughter Kathleen. The bakery was bombed during the Second World War. After the war John's son Peter rebuilt the bakehouse, installed new ovens and remodelled the shop front. The shop, still owned and run by the Newens family, is a bakery as well as a restaurant and tea room, and the maids of honour are still served – made to a closely kept secret recipe.

Curiously, as here, some recipes omit the cheese altogether, replacing it with ground almonds, flour or other thickening ingredients. One example is a lemon cheesecake created in the late seventeenth century, its filling consisting of pounded lemon peel, egg yolks, sugar and butter. This mixture is still known today in England as 'lemon curd' or 'lemon cheese' and is sold in jars as a preserve.

ST CLEMENT'S TARTS

225g/8oz shortcrust (pie) pastry
75g/3oz/¾ stick butter
75g/3oz/3 tablespoons golden caster (milled golden
*   cane) sugar*
2 eggs, separated
grated zest and juice of 1 orange
grated zest and 1 tablespoon juice of 1 lemon

Preheat the oven to 200°C/400°F/gas mark 6.
Roll out the pastry and line 10–12 patty or tartlet
tins. Cream the butter and sugar until light, then
gradually beat in the egg yolks. Slowly stir in the
zest and juices until blended. Whisk the egg
whites until stiff and fold into the mixture. Pour
into the pastry cases and cook for about 25
minutes. Cool on a wire rack.

St Clement's denotes the combination of orange and
lemon flavours. This derives from the ancient custom at St
Clement's Inn in London of giving these fruit to the poor.
The old nursery rhyme commemorates this with the lines,
'Oranges and lemons/Say the bells of St Clement's.'
Citrus fruits were encountered by the Crusaders in the
twelfth century. A century later lemons, oranges and
pomegranates were shipped to England at great expense.
In Elizabethan times oranges and lemons were used in
puddings, pies, cakes and jams. By the eighteenth century
they were imported in large quantities and their juice was
a key ingredient in sauces served with meat and fish.

ECCLES CAKES

Homemade Eccles cakes are delightful. Packed with currants and candied peel and scented with spices, they are much nicer than the rather dry pre-packed ones on supermarket shelves.

225g/8oz puff pastry

for the filling
50g/2oz/½ stick butter
110g/4oz/¾ cup currants
50g/2oz/½ cup candied peel, finely chopped
1 teaspoon ground mixed spice (pumpkin spice)
25g/1oz/1 tablespoon light muscovado (light brown muscovado) sugar
milk and golden granulated (milled golden cane) sugar to glaze

Preheat the oven to 230°C/450°F/gas mark 8. Place all the ingredients for the filling into a small pan and heat gently until the sugar has dissolved and the butter melted. Mix well and leave to cool. Roll out the pastry thinly and cut into 10cm/4in rounds. Put a large teaspoonful of the mixture in the centre of each round and fold in the edges to enclose the mixture. Turn the pastry rounds over and press gently with a rolling pin to flatten them. Cut 3 slits in the top of each cake and place on a greased baking tray. Brush with milk and sprinkle with sugar. Bake for about 15 minutes until golden (the currants will bulge through the pastry). These are best eaten fresh and warm.

The old meaning of the word 'eccles' was church and it is probable that these fruity, buttery cakes had a religious significance, most likely being eaten at Christmas. The fruits and spices were luxury items and eaten on special occasions. In the twelfth century, on their return to England, the Crusaders introduced the small pastry cakes filled with fruit and spices which they had enjoyed in the East.

How and why the cakes became particularly associated with the town of Eccles in Lancashire is something of a mystery. However, the people of Eccles continued to make the cakes secretly after the Puritans banned the eating of such things at religious festivals. Later on the cakes were associated with the fairs or 'wakes' in the area. Some very old recipes use mint leaves as well as the fruit and spices.

SOFT MOIST CHOCOLATE CAKE

150ml/5fl oz/generous ½ cup sunflower oil
150ml/5fl oz/generous ½ cup plain yoghurt
5 tablespoons Seville orange marmalade
175g/6oz/1 cup dark muscovado (dark brown
    molasses) sugar
3 eggs
225g/8oz/2 cups self-raising (self-rising) flour
2 tablespoons cocoa powder
½ teaspoon bicarbonate of soda (baking soda)

for the topping
175g/6oz milk or plain (semi-sweet) chocolate
50g/2oz/½ stick butter

Preheat the oven to 170°C/325°F/gas mark 3. Beat together the oil, yoghurt, marmalade, sugar and eggs in a large bowl. In another bowl, sift together the dry ingredients and beat into the cake mixture. Spoon into a greased, lined 20cm/8in round, deep cake tin and bake for 1½–1¾ hours until a skewer comes out clean. Cool in the tin for 10 minutes, then turn out on to a wire rack and leave to become cold. To make the topping, melt the chocolate and butter in a bowl over hot (not boiling) water and cool until thickened. Spoon over the cake and spread with a knife to give a swirled effect.

CHOCOLATE:
A BRIEF HISTORY

The English love affair with chocolate began in London in 1657, when a Frenchman opened the country's first chocolate house in Queen's Head Alley in Bishopsgate, advertising 'this excellent West India drink'. Costing between ten and fifteen shillings per 450g/1lb, chocolate was considered a beverage for the wealthy elite. Samuel Pepys drank it for the first time in 1662 and must have enjoyed the experience, because his diary mentions more visits to chocolate houses and he writes several times of 'my morning draft of chocollatte'.

The most famous chocolate house was White's in fashionable St James's Street, opened in 1693 by an Italian immigrant named Francis White. The chocolate drinks, served along with ale, beer, snacks and coffee, were made from blocks of solid cocoa, probably imported from Spain. Pressed cakes from which the drink could be made at home were also sold there. But by the end of the eighteenth century London's chocolate houses began to disappear, many of the more fashionable ones becoming smart gentlemen's clubs. White's remains an exclusive gentlemen's club today.

A major turning point for the chocolate industry occurred in 1847, when Fry's of England made the first solid edible chocolate bar. Chocolate was an expensive luxury. In her famous *Book of Household Management* of 1861 Mrs Beeton instructed that chocolate should be served in an ornamental box placed on a glass plate as part of the dessert. Gradually, though, chocolate became more affordable and so within the reach of a wider section of the population.

WEST COUNTRY CIDER CAKE

Reducing the cider for this recipe greatly improves the flavour of the finished cake.

300ml/10fl oz/1¼ cups medium or sweet cider
110g/4oz/1 stick butter
110g/4oz/½ cup golden caster (milled golden cane) sugar
2 eggs, beaten
225g/8oz/2 cups plain (all-purpose) flour
1 teaspoon baking powder
little freshly grated nutmeg

Preheat the oven to 190°C/375°F/gas mark 5. In a small pan heat the cider until boiling, then lower the heat and simmer gently until reduced by half. Remove from the heat and leave until cold. Cream the butter and sugar until light and gradually beat in the eggs. Sift in the flour and baking powder, and fold in until well mixed. Gently stir in the nutmeg and cold cider. Spoon into a 20cm/8in greased, lined round cake tin and bake for 30–40 minutes until cooked through.

The West Country is famous for its apple orchards and cider. Although cider was known in England before the Norman invasion in 1066, large quantities were still imported from Normandy. Around this time vast orchards were planted in Sussex and Kent to make cider and the popularity of the drink spread throughout England, particularly in the West Country.

HONEY CAKE

Try using different types of honey to subtly change the flavour of this deliciously moist cake. The flavour, colour and texture of honey vary enormously from pale, thick and creamy, through golden amber, to the richly aromatic, almost black, liquid varieties. Each honey has its own unique flavour, depending on which flowers the bees have visited. Acacia honey, for instance, is clear, pale and very sweet with a heavily scented flavour and a runny consistency, while heather honey is rich reddish-brown in colour, with a dense texture and a not too sweet flavour that has a hint of bitter caramel.

300ml/10fl oz/1¼ cups dark honey
75g/3oz/¾ stick butter
350g/12oz/3 cups wholemeal (whole wheat) flour
2 teaspoons mixed spice (pumpkin spice)
1 teaspoon bicarbonate of soda (baking soda)
50g/2oz/½ cup candied orange peel, chopped finely
3 eggs
3 tablespoons milk
finely grated zest of 1 orange

Preheat the oven to 170°C/325°F/gas mark 3. Spoon out 4 tablespoons honey and set aside. Put the rest of the honey into a small pan with the butter and heat gently until just melted. Sift the flour, spice and bicarbonate of soda (baking soda) into a large bowl and stir in the candied peel. Beat the eggs, milk and orange zest and add to the dry ingredients with the cooled honey mixture. Beat until well mixed and pour into a greased, lined 20cm/8in square tin or 18cm/7in round, deep cake tin. Bake for about 1½ hours until cooked through. Leave to cool in the tin for 5 minutes, then turn out on to a wire rack. Prick the top of the cake with a skewer or fork and brush with the reserved honey while the cake is still warm. When cold, wrap in greaseproof (waxed) paper or non-stick baking paper and keep in an airtight tin for a few days before eating to allow the flavours to develop.

HONEY IN COOKING

Before the discovery of sugar, honey's main use was to sweeten foods. It was also an important ingredient in cooking and brewing. Honey beer and mead were the staple drinks throughout Britain and Ireland in ancient times. Honey has been used in cookery for thousands of years – honey cakes were found in a 5,000-year-old Egyptian tomb! Moulded, spiced honey cakes were made in monasteries and convents throughout Europe to celebrate saints' days and other religious feasts, as honey cakes retained their shape and the carved detail of the moulds well. Cakes made with honey are moist and keep remarkably well.

It is best to buy organic honey or a good-quality honey that hasn't been filtered or heat-treated, as these processes remove valuable enzymes and nutrients. Feeding the bees on a sugar and water solution placed near the hives is a method used to produce cheaper honeys, but this short cut means that the enzyme action doesn't occur. Health shops, small local beekeepers, honey farms, local markets and farm shops are the best sources of good-quality honeys. Keep the jar tightly sealed in a dry place. Honey will keep indefinitely, although it will crystallise during long storage or if it becomes too cold. If this happens, just stand the jar in hot water for a few minutes and the honey will become liquid again.

RICH DARK GINGERBREAD

A traditional gingerbread that's just how it should be – rich, dark and sticky. Marmalade, dried fruits and stem ginger add another dimension to the flavour here. In Yorkshire, gingerbread is sometimes eaten with butter or cheese. It makes a great pudding too, served with whipped cream or ice cream.

225g/8oz/2 sticks butter
225g/8oz/1¼ cups molasses (dark brown molasses)
  sugar
300ml/10fl oz/1¼ cups milk
225g/8oz/¾ cup marmalade (Seville, ginger,
  tangerine, etc.)
375g/12oz/3 cups self-raising (self-rising) flour
1 tablespoon ground ginger
2 teaspoons ground cinnamon
1 teaspoon grated nutmeg
½ teaspoon ground mixed spice (pumpkin spice)
2 teaspoons bicarbonate of soda (baking soda)
2 eggs, beaten
7 pieces stem ginger, chopped
110g/4oz/¾ cup sultanas (golden raisins) or raisins

Preheat the oven to 150°C/300°F/gas mark 2. Melt together the butter, sugar, milk and marmalade in a pan over a low heat, then leave to cool. Mix the dry ingredients together in a large bowl and make a hollow in the centre. Slowly pour in the melted mixture, stirring all the time, to form a smooth batter. Beat in the eggs, then stir in the stem ginger and sultanas (golden raisins) or raisins. Pour into a greased, lined 23cm/9in cake tin and bake for 1½–2 hours until risen and firm in the centre. Cool in the tin. This tastes even better if kept, well wrapped, in an airtight tin for 2 days before eating.

Gingerbread is an ancient spiced cake and every county has its own particular recipe, varying from crisp cream-coloured biscuits (cookies) to dark, moist and sticky slabs of cake. In medieval England, gingerbread (the word is a corruption of Old French *gingebras*, meaning 'preserved ginger') was made by mixing stale bread-crumbs with honey and spices, colouring it red with sanders or saunders (a variety of sandalwood) and pressing the mixture into moulds to dry out in a cool oven. It was a very popular and important item at fairs in the late Middle Ages and for centuries after. For special occasions it was gilded with gold leaf (the proverbial gilt on the gingerbread) and studded with cloves. White gingerbread was something of a misnomer, as it was marzipan flavoured with ginger and then gilded. Legend has it that the perennial children's favourites, gingerbread men, were created when Elizabeth I ordered her cooks to make caricatures of her courtiers. London street sellers of the eighteenth century would cry, 'Hot gingerbread, smoking hot!', selling it from carts complete with a little furnace and chimney.

CARROT AND GINGER CAKE

A lovely soft, moist cake with the warmth of aromatic ginger.

110g/4oz/1 stick butter
75g/3oz/½ cup light muscovado (light brown muscovado) sugar
110g/4oz/1 cup self-raising (self-rising) flour
1 teaspoon baking powder
2 eggs
3 pieces stem ginger, chopped finely
2 tablespoons stem ginger syrup
110g/4oz carrots, grated
2 tablespoons ground almonds

Preheat the oven to 180°C/350°F/gas mark 4. Whiz the butter, sugar, flour, baking powder and eggs together in a food processor until smooth, then add the rest of the ingredients and process briefly until well mixed. Alternatively, beat the butter and sugar together until light, then gradually beat in the rest of the ingredients. Put into a 450g/1lb loaf tin lined with non-stick baking paper. Smooth the top and make a hollow in the centre. Bake for 55 minutes. If you like you can ice the top of the cake with 2–3 tablespoons of sifted golden icing (confectioner's) sugar mixed to a coating consistency with a little ginger syrup from the jar.

Root vegetables were commonly used in many sweet dishes – cakes, puddings, pies, tarts and preserves – their inherent natural sweetness and moist texture making them valuable ingredients. Carrots have the highest sugar content after sugar beet. The Tudors enjoyed sweet carrot puddings containing dried fruits and spices, and a vivid orange jam of the time was known as 'angel hair preserve'. Some old Christmas pudding recipes call for grated carrots – though this was originally an economy to lessen the amount of expensive sugar and dried fruits. During the Second World War, when sugar was often unavailable, carrots were used as a substitute for apricots in Mock Apricot Flan (a recipe issued by the Ministry of Food) and in apricot jam and orange marmalade, where they added bulk and colour as well as sweetness. Cakes made with carrots are beautifully moist and keep well.

MADEIRA CAKE

Madeira cake is firmer and richer than a sponge cake and contains no fruit or spices. Its name comes from the practice of eating a slice with a glass of Madeira malmsey wine. The cake remained popular and was a favourite of Victorian ladies.

175g/6oz/1½ sticks butter
175g/6oz/1 cup golden caster (milled golden cane) sugar
110g/4oz/1 cup plain (all-purpose) flour
110g/4oz/1 cup self-raising (self-rising) flour
grated zest of 1 small lemon
4 eggs, beaten
2–3 thin slices candied citron peel

Preheat the oven to 180°C/350°F/gas mark 4. Beat the butter and sugar together until light and creamy. Sift in the flours, add the lemon zest and mix well. Gradually beat in the eggs until the mixture is smooth. Turn into a greased and lined 18cm/7in deep, round cake tin and bake for 30 minutes. Arrange the citron slices carefully on top of the cake and continue baking for another 30 minutes until well risen and firm. Cool in the tin for a few minutes, then turn out and finish cooling on a wire rack.

SAFFRON CAKE

The world's most expensive spice, saffron is available in both filaments and powder, though the vibrant deep orange-red filaments are preferable to the powder as the latter can easily be adulterated.

300ml/10fl oz/1¼ cups milk
½ teaspoon saffron strands
450g/1lb/4 cups plain (all-purpose) flour
pinch of salt
¼ teaspoon bicarbonate of soda (baking soda)
225g/8oz/2 sticks butter
50g/2oz/½ cup candied peel, chopped
175g/6oz/1 cup currants
175g/6oz/¾ cup golden caster (milled golden cane)
     sugar
2 eggs, beaten

Heat the milk. When hot, pour on to the saffron strands. Leave to stand for at least 2 hours. Preheat the oven to 180°C/350°F/gas mark 4. Sift the flour, salt and bicarbonate of soda (baking soda) into a bowl and rub in the butter until the mixture resembles breadcrumbs. Add the peel, currants and sugar. Mix well. Stir in the eggs. Strain in the saffron milk and beat well. Turn the mixture into a greased, lined 23cm/9in deep round cake tin. Bake for 1½–2 hours until a skewer inserted into the centre of the cake comes out clean. Cool in the tin for 10 minutes. Turn out on to a wire rack to cool.

THE STORY OF SAFFRON

Since antiquity saffron has been one of the most expensive and sought-after spices in the world. Its warm, evocative aroma perfumed the palaces of Egyptian pharaohs and the leaders of ancient Greece and Rome. The Romans scattered it around theatres and other public places as a fumigant – the streets of Rome were sprinkled with saffron when Nero made his entry into the city. Cleopatra valued it as an aphrodisiac. The Phoenicians offered honeyed saffron cakes to their gods.

The name is Middle Eastern in origin, combining the words *sahafarn* (thread) and *za'faran* (yellow) to make saffron. The thread-like filaments are the dried stigmas of a flowering plant, *Crocus sativus Linneaus*, which belongs to the family Iridaceae. The beautiful purple flowers bear red stigmas and yellow stamens. Each flower contains only three stigmas. The stigmas contain crocin, the source of saffron's strong colouring property, bitter-crocin, which gives saffron its distinctive aroma and taste, and a tiny amount of essential oil picrocrocin, which is responsible for saffron's therapeutic properties. The yellow-orange stigmas are removed by hand and then dried over a low heat, which reduces their weight by about 80 per cent. The filaments or threads are packaged whole in sealed containers in order to guarantee their purity as well as to protect their strong, slightly bitter aroma.

Legend has it that saffron was introduced to England by returning Crusaders in the fourteenth century. Cultivation centred on Saffron Walden in Essex but died out in the fifteenth century, when saffron began to be cultivated in herb gardens. To meet the demand the spice had to be imported from the East. The warm aroma and brilliant golden colour have been used to colour and flavour foods in England for centuries.

Only a small amount is needed to flavour a dish – too much and the end result will have a distinctly 'medicinal' flavour. Add the threads to a small cup of hot water and let them infuse for about 15 minutes, then add them with the liquid to the dish to ensure a uniform colour.

CARAWAY SEED CAKE

An old-fashioned cake, whose distinctive pungent, almost lemony flavour many people will remember from childhood teas with elderly aunts.

175g/6oz/1½ sticks butter
175g/6oz/¾ cup golden caster (milled golden cane) sugar
1–2 dessertspoons caraway seeds, lightly crushed
3 eggs, separated
large pinch each of ground cinnamon and nutmeg (optional)
225g/8oz/2 cups self-raising (self-rising) flour
milk to mix

Preheat the oven to 180°C/350°F/gas mark 4. Cream the butter and sugar until pale and light, then stir in the caraway seeds. Whisk the egg whites until stiff but not dry and gently beat in the egg yolks until well blended. Add to the creamed mixture with the spices, if using, and sift in the flour. Pour in a little milk if necessary to achieve a soft dropping consistency. Tip into a greased, lined 900g/2lb loaf tin and smooth the top. Bake for just over 1 hour until cooked through. Cool in the tin for 20 minutes, then turn out on to a wire rack to cool completely.

Caraway seed cake dates back to the sixteenth century, when the caraway seeds would have been coated in sugar and called 'comfits'. The plain seeds began to be used in cakes in the seventeenth and eighteenth centuries. 'Seed cake' was mentioned in Charles Dickens's *David Copperfield* (1858) and was popular at that time. The cake was a great favourite at harvest time in Yorkshire. Curiously, it was thought that eating caraway seeds imparted strength and also prevented a person from stealing! Consequently, astute farmers made sure that the seeds were included in as many foods as possible, such as breads and cheeses as well as the cake.

PORTER CAKE

For hundreds of years both rich and poor alike enjoyed beer with meals and households used brewer's yeast to make bread until the development of baker's yeast in the mid-nineteenth century. This speeded up the process and tasted better than brewer's yeast. Porter is ideal for this rich, dark fruitcake, but you can use any strong dark beer. Serve sliced with butter and/or cheese if liked.

225g/8oz/2 sticks butter
225g/8oz/1¼ cups dark muscovado (dark brown molasses) sugar
3 eggs
350g/12oz/3 cups plain (all-purpose) flour
1 teaspoon baking powder
1 teaspoon mixed spice (pumpkin spice)
450g/1lb/3 cups raisins and currants, mixed
50g/2oz/½ cup walnuts, chopped
150ml/5fl oz/generous ½ cup porter or stout
2 tablespoons dark rum (optional)

Preheat the oven to 170°C/325°F/gas mark 3. Cream the butter and sugar until light and fluffy. Beat in the eggs, one at a time, then sift in the flour, baking powder and spice. Add the dried fruits and walnuts, followed by the porter and rum, if using. Put into a greased, lined 20cm/8in round, deep cake tin and bake for 1 hour, then reduce the oven temperature 150°C/300°F/gas mark 2 and bake for another 1–2 hours until cooked through. Remove from the oven and leave to cool in the tin for about 30 minutes before turning out.

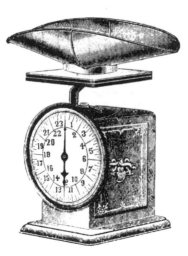

YORKSHIRE CURD TART

Curd cheese has a mild, tangy flavour. If you can't find curd cheese, substitute cottage cheese instead but it must be sieved first. The result will not be as rich, but it will still taste delicious!

225g/8oz shortcrust (pie) pastry
50g/2oz/½ stick butter
350g/12oz/2 cups soft curd cheese
75g/3oz/3 tablespoons golden caster (milled golden cane) sugar
2 eggs
1 tablespoon rum or brandy (optional)
2 tablespoons single (light) cream
pinch of ground mixed spice (pumpkin spice)
50g/2oz/2 tablespoons currants or raisins
grated nutmeg

Preheat the oven to 180°C/350°F/gas mark 4. Line a 20cm/8in flan tin with pastry. Prick the base with a fork and bake 'blind' for 25 minutes. Leave to cool. Cream the butter, cheese and sugar until smooth, then beat in the eggs, rum or brandy, if using, cream and mixed spice (pumpkin spice). Stir in the currants or raisins and put the mixture into the pastry case. Grate a little nutmeg over the top and bake for 40 minutes. You can serve the tarts warm or cold.

Cheesecakes, first mentioned in the Middle Ages, were popular treats sold at summer fairs. The earliest recipe for cheesecake made with soft cheese is in the first real English cookery book, *Forme of Cury*, of 1390 (*cury* was the Old English word for cooking, derived from the French *cuire*, meaning 'to cook, boil or grill'). Cheesecakes were a perfect way of using up the surplus curds produced by sour milk and each region developed its own type of cheesecake. Melton Mowbray produced such huge numbers of cheesecakes for the annual Whitsuntide fair that it was said there were enough to pave the entire town!

Yorkshire became particularly renowned for its creamy curd tarts, which are still made today by the county's bakers. In the past the tarts appeared on farmhouse tea tables and housewives baked them specially for communal feasts held on special occasions and religious holidays. Over time other ingredients, such as brandy, rum and candied peel, were added to the basic recipe. The type of modern cheesecake that has an uncooked cream cheese filling on a biscuit (cookie) crumb base is an American invention that differs greatly from English cheesecakes, which traditionally include dried fruits and spices and are baked in the oven.

WALNUT AND HONEY TART

Buy organic or a good-quality honey for the best results. Commercially produced blended honey comes from mixed flower honeys around the world and has a uniformly bland flavour that is intended to appeal to a mass market.

175g/6oz/1¼ cups plain (all-purpose) flour
pinch of salt
75g/3oz/¾ stick butter
grated rind and juice of 1 large orange
4 tablespoons honey
75g/3oz/generous cup fresh wholemeal (whole wheat)
    breadcrumbs
3 tablespoons dark muscovado (dark brown molasses)
    sugar
3 eggs
110g/4oz/1 cup walnuts, chopped roughly

Preheat the oven to 200°C/400°F/gas mark 4. Sift the flour and salt into a bowl and rub in the butter until the mixture resembles breadcrumbs. Stir in the orange rind and enough juice to form a soft dough. Line a 20cm/8in flan tin with the pastry and bake 'blind' for 10–15 minutes. Mix together the honey, breadcrumbs and sugar. Gradually beat in the eggs and any remaining orange juice. Scatter the walnuts over the base of the pastry case and pour over the filling. Bake for 20–25 minutes until cooked through. If the tart is browning too fast during this time, cover with foil. Cool in the tin for 15 minutes, then finish cooling on a wire rack.

The Romans introduced walnut trees to England. They were cultivated in medieval orchards and, after picking, the nuts in their shells were stored buried in earth or salt to preserve them. Walnuts were eaten after a meal to 'close' the stomach. In 1597 John Gerard wrote in his *Herball*, '. . . the greene and tender Nuts boyled in Sugar eaten as Suckad, are a most pleasant and delectable meat, comfort the stomacke, and expel poison'. Planted in great numbers in English parks and gardens, walnut trees were valued not only for their rich, crisp-textured nuts, but also for their excellent wood. When young and fresh, walnuts have a deliciously milky flavour and a better texture than the rather woody, sometimes bitter specimens on offer today in the shops.

BATH BUNS

Commercially produced Bath buns often contain fruit and artificial colouring and tend to be overly sweet. This recipe is similar to the original, which was very like a brioche.

300ml/10fl oz/1¼ cups lukewarm milk
15g/½oz fresh yeast
450g/1lb/4 cups plain (all-purpose) flour
1 teaspoon salt
2 tablespoons golden caster (milled golden cane)
    sugar
225g/8oz/2 sticks butter
extra milk and sugar for glazing
2 tablespoons roughly crushed sugar cubes or candy
    sugar

Place half the milk and the yeast in a small cup and leave until frothy. Sieve the flour, salt and sugar into a warmed bowl and rub in the butter. Stir in the yeast mixture and mix to a light dough, adding extra milk if necessary. Cover the bowl and leave in a warm place for about 1½ hours until the dough has risen and is light and puffy. Preheat the oven to 190°C/375°F/gas mark 5. Place tablespoons of the dough on to buttered, floured baking trays, smoothing the top of each bun with a knife. Cover with a clean tea towel and leave for about 15 minutes. Bake the buns for

15–20 minutes until puffed up and almost joined together. Heat the milk and sugar until boiling and use to brush the tops of the buns. Immediately sprinkle with crushed sugar.

BATH BUNS

Bath became the fashionable place to be after the visit of Queen Anne in 1702. The 'beau monde' of the day flocked to spend their summers there, attending the theatre, parties and concerts, drinking the waters in the Pump Room and visiting the famous baths. They followed a strict code of etiquette laid down by Beau Nash, the fashionable dandy of the time.

Bath buns, still made in Bath today, are slightly flat and bumpy yeast buns topped with a sticky glaze and crushed sugar. Their origin is obscure but they are thought to have first been made in the eighteenth century, when they were originally topped with caraway seeds and sugar nibs, but with the passing of time, currants have replaced the caraway seeds. The roughly crushed sugar was taken from the only form of sugar available then – a sugar loaf shaped like a conical hat and weighing about 6kg/13lb. Enormous sugar cutters were used to break the sugar into large pieces, which were then further reduced to smaller lumps with more delicate cutters. Authentic Bath buns are made from very rich plain dough, with no fruit added. The first reference to them comes from Jane Austen, when she wrote in January 1801 of 'disordering my Stomach with Bath bunns'.

SALLY LUNNS

15g/½oz fresh yeast
4 tablespoons lukewarm milk
450g/1lb/4 cups strong (bread) flour
2 teaspoons salt
1 teaspoon ground mixed spice (pumpkin spice)
250g/9oz/2 cups thick double (heavy) cream, at room
   temperature
4 eggs, beaten

for the glaze
2 tablespoons sugar
2 tablespoons milk

Put the yeast and tepid milk into a cup and leave for a few minutes until frothy. Meanwhile, mix the flour, salt and spice in a large bowl. Add the yeast mixture, cream and eggs, and mix until thick and just stiff enough to form into shape. Halve the dough and form each half into a ball. Place the balls of dough into a buttered, floured 15cm/6in tin about 7.5cm/3in deep and sprinkle each lightly with flour. Cover and leave in a warm place until the dough has risen to the tops of the tin. This will take between 1½ and 2 hours. Meanwhile, preheat the oven to 200°C/400°F/ gas mark 6. When the dough has risen, place the cake tin in the oven and bake for 15 minutes until golden. Heat the milk and sugar for the glaze in a small pan until boiling. Brush the top of the cakes with this mixture while still in the tin. Cool in the tin for a few minutes, then turn out and split the cakes in half. Spread with clotted cream or butter, replace the tops and eat while warm. Alternatively leave plain and eat with ice cream or a fruit dessert. Delicious toasted and buttered.

Sally Lunn, a Huguenot pastry cook fleeing from persecution in France, is reputed to have started a bakery in 1680 in Bath's oldest house in Lilliput Alley, which was built in 1482 and was previously the home of the Dukes of Kingston. Sally Lunn, it is said, used to cry her wares in the city's streets. The bakery became famous for its teacakes and was patronised by Beau Nash and other notables of the day. Today the bakery survives as a popular tea shop and the delicious teacakes are still made there to a closely guarded secret recipe, which came with the deeds of the house. The building was extensively renovated in the 1930s, when the original ovens were discovered in the basement. These, together with the original foot trough in which large quantities of dough were pounded, can be seen today – although this is one part of the original recipe which is no longer adhered to!

An alternative theory is that the name of the teacakes derives from *soleil lune* ('sun' and 'moon') cakes, because the cakes were round and golden on top and pale underneath.

CHELSEA BUNS

These are scrumptious eaten at teatime or breakfast – in fact at any time of the day!

175ml/6fl oz/¾ cup milk
50g/2oz/½ stick butter
450g/1lb/4 cups strong white (bread) flour
1 teaspoon salt
50g/2oz/2 tablespoons golden caster (milled golden cane) sugar, plus extra for sprinkling
1 × 7g/¼oz sachet easy-blend (fast action) yeast
2 medium eggs, beaten

for the filling
50g/2oz/½ stick butter
75g/3oz/½ cup light muscovado (light brown muscovado) sugar
75g/3oz/½ cup raisins
1 teaspoon ground cinnamon

for the glaze
4 tablespoons milk
3 tablespoons golden caster (milled golden cane) sugar

Heat the milk and butter in a pan until the butter has melted, but don't allow it to become hot. Remove from the heat. Sift the flour into a large mixing bowl and stir in the salt, golden caster (milled golden cane) sugar and yeast. Make a well in the centre and pour in the warm milk mixture and the eggs. Work to a soft dough that leaves the sides of the bowl clean. Turn out on to a floured surface and knead for about 7 minutes until smooth and elastic. Place the dough in an oiled bowl and cover with cling film (plastic wrap). Leave in a warm place for 1–2 hours until doubled in size. Turn out and knead lightly. Roll out to a rectangle approximately 35 × 28cm/14 × 11in. Melt the butter for the filling and brush over the dough. Sprinkle the light muscovado (light brown muscovado) sugar, raisins and cinnamon over the dough, leaving a gap around the edges. Starting at the longer edge, roll up the dough carefully and trim off the ends. Cut into 9 even slices and arrange them next to each other in a 20cm/8in buttered square tin. Cover and leave for 30–40 minutes until puffy and slightly risen. Meanwhile, preheat the oven to 190°C/375°F/ gas mark 5. Sprinkle the buns with 1–2 tablespoons golden caster (milled golden cane) sugar and bake for about 30 minutes until well risen and browned. To make the glaze, heat the milk and sugar until the sugar has melted. Remove the buns from the oven and immediately brush 2 or 3 times with the glaze. Place on a wire rack to cool and pull the buns apart before serving them.

A HISTORY OF THE CHELSEA BUN

These sweet, spicy currant buns were first made at the Chelsea Bun House in Pimlico Road, London, in the late seventeenth or early eighteenth century, to feed the crowds of visitors who went there on Sunday afternoons. The owner, Richard Hand, was a flamboyant character known as Captain Bun. The Chelsea Bun House was patronised by royalty and interestingly also housed a museum of curiosities and antiquities. In addition to having royal patronage, it reportedly sold 240,000 buns on Good Friday 1829, but sadly this could not prevent its demise. It was demolished in 1839 and its collection of curiosities sold at auction.

Cambridge's most popular bakery, Fitzbillies, was opened in the early 1920s among the university colleges in the centre of town. Students, dons and townspeople would form long queues there daily to buy the renowned soft, rich and wonderfully moist Chelsea buns. Needless to say, subsequent owners have jealously guarded the secret recipe.

SEASONAL
CELEBRATIONS

Here, you'll find a collection of traditional recipes to mark special occasions year round. But when it comes to seasonal celebrations, for most people Christmas is the big one.

The familiar warm, spicy fragrance and rich, fruity flavours of today's traditional English Christmas fare are a distant echo from our medieval past. Recipes have survived through the centuries, frequently undergoing intervention and adaptation to meet tastes.

Costly new and luxurious foodstuffs in the form of dried fruits, spices, sugar, almonds and citrus fruits were imported from exotic lands in vast quantities. Such foods were fashionable status symbols among a rich and self-indulgent elite and were used lavishly in the great feasts of the time, particularly at Christmas.

These were spectacular events in the Middle Ages, depending on the wealth of the host. Richard II's Yuletide feast was said to have catered for 10,000 people daily. The walls of the great hall where the feast was held (the word banquet didn't come into use until after the medieval period) were hung with rich tapestries and sweet-smelling herbs were strewn on the floor. Beautiful cloths, sometimes of silk, covered the tables. Entertainments were an important part of the festivities, with minstrels, jugglers, acrobats, jesters and mummers performing throughout.

The general public were allowed to crowd into the hall or the gallery to watch the proceedings from a respectful distance and the leftovers from each course were collected and distributed among them. They must surely have been awestruck by the array of fabulous delicacies. Christmas afforded them a rare opportunity to taste such exotic delights.

One of the chief skills of the medieval cook was the ability to transform simple ingredients into exotic works of art. The jewel-bright food dyes were obtained from herbs, plants and spices: red from sunders or saunders (a variety of sandalwood) or alkanet (a variety of borage); green from mint or spinach juice; blue from mulberry juice or a darker blue from the indigo plant; yellow from saffron; purple from turnsole (a Mediterranean plant); and black from boiled animal blood. Gold and silver leaf was used to gild foods at important feasts. Black and white foods were in vogue, the latter being considered particularly fashionable. Finished dishes were often multicoloured: for instance, striped jellies or large chequered custard tarts which were divided into sections, each a different colour. Further embellishments were added in the form of red and white aniseed or caraway comfits (sugar-coated seeds), pomegranate seeds or powdered spices.

After the digestant, spicy sweetmeats and spiced sweetened alcoholic drinks, the feast was over. The splendid foods of these Yuletide medieval feasts set the pattern for many future Christmases.

ROAST TURKEY

The turkey should be at room temperature when it goes into the oven, so take it out of the refrigerator in plenty of time.

Place the turkey breast-side up in a roasting tin. Sprinkle with salt and pepper and brush with melted butter or oil. Add 110ml/4fl oz/½ cup water to the bottom of the roasting pan. Place the turkey in a preheated oven 170°C/ 325°F/gas mark 3. A 2.7–3.6kg/6–8lb bird will need 2–3 hours; a 3.6–6.3kg/8–14lb bird will need 3–4 hours. Juices from the turkey will baste the meat as it cooks, so there is no need to baste during the cooking time. If the turkey is becoming too brown before it is cooked, loosely cover it with foil and continue cooking. If you have a meat thermometer, make sure that turkey reaches 82°C/180°F in the innermost portion of the thigh, not touching any bone, before removing it from the oven. Remove the bird from the oven, and allow it to stand for 20 minutes before carving. This allows the juices to redistribute for easier carving.

FESTIVE DISHES

The centrepieces of a medieval Christmas feast were dishes designed to amuse and entertain, usually a roast swan or peacock splendidly arrayed in full plumage, complete with gilded beak and adorned with a silver or gold crown. Boar's head was also served at Christmas, glazed with aspic jelly and garlanded with herbs and leaves, its tusks gilded with gold leaf, and made an impressive centrepiece. Every type of fish, meat and poultry was accompanied by its own particular sauce and it was the duty of the servers to ensure that the correct sauces were provided in the small dishes (saucers) placed along the length of the table. For example, mustard sauce accompanied boar's head, while ginger sauce accompanied pheasant or partridge.

Turkeys first arrived in England in the sixteenth century – Archbishop Cranmer provided the first written record of turkey in 1541. As time passed the birds became popular and cheaper, eventually ousting the peacocks and swans that had traditionally been served at grand medieval feasts. They became farmyard fowl and in the seventeenth and eighteenth centuries great numbers of them were walked considerable distances to the London markets. Journeys from Norfolk and Suffolk could start as early as September, after the harvest, and take three months.

CHESTNUT AND BACON STUFFING

Chestnut stuffings were popular in the eighteenth century. A large bird such as a turkey is stuffed to prevent the meat from drying out during the long cooking. This recipe will stuff a 5-6 kg/11–13lb turkey.

25g/1oz/¼ stick butter
1 large onion, finely chopped
110g/4oz streaky (slab) bacon, diced
450g/1lb tinned or vacuum-packed chestnuts, finely chopped
2 tablespoons chopped fresh parsley
1 tablespoon chopped fresh thyme
1 teaspoon chopped fresh sage
grated zest of 1 lemon
2 tablespoons fresh white breadcrumbs
pinch of ground mace
225g/8oz pork sausage meat
1 egg, beaten
salt and pepper

Preheat the oven to 170°C/325°F/gas mark 3. Heat the butter in a frying pan and add the onion and bacon. Cook for 10 minutes, then remove from the heat and mix with the remaining ingredients. Spoon into a buttered ovenproof baking dish and cook for about 45 minutes.

BREAD SAUCE

Many traditional recipes from medieval times are still in use today. In the Middle Ages bread sauce was served as an accompaniment to veal and venison. Bread was beaten with the meat juices and spices until smooth and thick. Bread sauce spiced with mace, cloves and pepper is traditionally served with roast chicken or turkey, especially at Christmas.

1 medium-sized onion, peeled and quartered
2 whole cloves
600ml/1 pint/2½ cups milk
2 blades mace
tiny pinch grated nutmeg
6 black peppercorns
1 bay leaf, crushed
110g/4oz/2 cups fresh white breadcrumbs
salt and pepper
25g/1oz/¼ stick butter
1–2 tablespoons double (heavy) cream

Stud the onion with the cloves. Put into a pan with the milk, spices and bay leaves, and heat very gently until the milk comes to the boil. Remove from the heat, cover and leave to stand for 4–5 hours. Strain the milk into a bowl and return to the pan. Add the breadcrumbs and heat very gently until the breadcrumbs have swollen. Beat well until smooth. Season to taste, then stir in the butter and cream. Serve immediately.

TRADITIONAL ROAST GOOSE

Goose is by far the tastiest of all domesticated fowl. The fat just underneath the skin melts into the flesh, so that the goose cooks to a rich succulence with a slightly gamey flavour without needing any attention, effectively basting itself. Goose fat also makes superbly crisp, crunchy roast potatoes and excellent pastry. A 5kg/11lb bird will feed 6 people generously. An oven-ready frozen goose should be thoroughly thawed slowly in the refrigerator before cooking Prick the bird all over before roasting to allow the fat to escape and pour off the accumulated fat from time to time during cooking. After an initial blast of heat, roast the goose for 20 minutes per 450g/1lb, plus 20 minutes, in a moderate oven – 180°C/350°F/gas mark 4. It is cooked when the juices run pale gold – test it with a skewer in the thigh.

5kg/11lb oven-ready goose
1 small lemon, halved
1 teaspoon salt

for the stuffing
900g/2lb freshly boiled potatoes, drained
1 onion, finely chopped
4 rashers bacon, finely chopped
1 teaspoon salt

½ teaspoon pepper
75g/3oz/¾ stick butter
1 tablespoon chopped fresh sage
1 tablespoon chopped fresh parsley
1 tablespoon chopped fresh thyme

Preheat the oven to 200°C/400°F/gas mark 6. Prick the goose all over and rub the skin with a lemon half. Squeeze the juice of the other half into the cavity of the goose. Rub the skin with the salt. Mash the potatoes and mix with the rest of the stuffing ingredients. Stuff the goose loosely with the mixture (don't overfill the bird as the stuffing will swell during cooking). Cook any surplus stuffing separately in a greased dish. Secure the tail end with skewers and truss the goose neatly with string to hold the wings and legs close to the body. Place on a rack in a large roasting tin (pan) and transfer to the oven. Cook for 30 minutes then reduce the temperature to 180°C/350°F/gas mark 4 and cook for a further 3–3½ hours until cooked through. Leave to rest for at least 15 minutes before carving.

COOKING THE GOOSE

'There never was such a goose . . . Its tenderness and flavour, size and cheapness were the themes of universal admiration.' So wrote Charles Dickens in *A Christmas Carol*, published in 1843.

In the Middle Ages, goose was regarded as the chief Christmas bird and, along with other fowl, was a popular Christmas gift. Gifts were given throughout the twelve days of Christmas, rather than just on Christmas Day.

After the harvest, geese were sent into the fields of stubble to graze on the grain left lying around and so were called 'stubble geese'. By the feast of St Michael the Archangel at Michaelmas (29 September), they were in prime condition and tenants paid their rent with a plump stubble goose. There was an old saying, dating back to the fifteenth century, that if you ate goose on Michaelmas Day you would never want for money the rest of the year. Almost every part of the goose appeared in some guise or other after Christmas Day: goose soup, giblet soup, pies and goose blood puddings, this last made by mixing goose blood with finely chopped onion, flour, oatmeal, salt, pepper and herbs.

MARMALADE-GLAZED HAM

Buy a good-quality piece of ham from a reputable butcher for the best flavour. Many excellent butchers now sell hams via mail order on the Internet, so there's really no need to make do with the bright pink, wet, flaccid ham joints sold in many supermarkets at Christmas.

approx. 1½–2 kg/3–4lb boned and rolled gammon
*   (ham) joint*
2 tablespoons Seville orange marmalade
finely grated zest and juice of 2 oranges
50g/2oz/¼ cup unrefined demerara sugar
2 tablespoons Dijon mustard

Soak the gammon in cold water for 12–24 hours if needed. (This isn't always necessary so check the directions on the pack). Preheat the oven to 170°C/325°F/gas mark 3. Place the joint in a large roasting bag or seal loosely in foil and put skin-side up in a large roasting tin (pan). Cook for 20 minutes per 450g/1lb, then 20 minutes before the end of the cooking time remove from the oven and increase the temperature to 220°C/ 425°F/gas mark 7. Mix the marmalade with the orange zest and juice, then the sugar.

Cut open the roasting bag or foil and, with a sharp knife, remove the rind from the joint, leaving the fat. Slash the fat diagonally into diamond shapes and spread first with the mustard and then with the orange mixture. Return to the oven for about 20 minutes until the glaze is bubbling. Remove from the oven and allow to stand for 15 minutes before slicing. This is also delicious eaten cold.

THE ORIGINS OF MARMALADE

A Portuguese quince preserve made from quinces, spices and sugar or honey (*marmelo* in Portuguese) was imported into England from Portugal in the fifteenth century and the first English reference to marmalade was in 1524. This early marmalade was dense and sticky, shaped into bricks and stored in boxes. It had a strong flavour and was served sliced as a dessert to honoured guests.

Gradually English housewives began to make their own marmalade. They continued to use quinces until the seventeenth century, when other fruits, such as lemons, grapefruit and oranges, gradually began to be used instead and the spices were omitted. Another innovation at this time was to include the thinly sliced peel of the fruit. It was also made with a looser texture and put into pots instead of boxes.

Around 1874, Sarah Jane, the wife of Oxford shopkeeper Frank Cooper, made the first batch of Frank Cooper's Marmalade for sale and was taken aback by the demand. Citrus fruits and sugar had become much cheaper and easily available and the confection soon became a standard item on English breakfast tables with sliced, toasted bread.

Along with jams, marmalade began to be made in small factories and many of these companies are still household names today. Its remarkable keeping qualities ensured that pots of it followed the British around the world. A tin was taken on Scott's expedition to the South Pole in 1910. Supplies were sent to royalty and dignitaries around the world, and travellers and explorers made sure it was included among their provisions.

Marmalade is an excellent ingredient in ice creams, pies, puddings and tarts. It also makes a wonderful sauce for duck and, as here, is a delicious glaze for a ham.

TURKEY AND CHESTNUT PIE

This creamy pie topped with light pastry is one of the best ways to use up leftover turkey.

50g/2oz/½ stick butter
1 large onion, finely chopped
1 bay leaf
1 clove garlic, finely chopped
450g/1lb chopped cooked turkey, white and dark meat
225g/8oz tinned unsweetened chestnuts, drained and halved
175g/6oz chestnut mushrooms, halved
40g/1½oz/1½ tablespoons plain (all-purpose) flour
600ml/1 pint/2½ cups chicken or turkey stock
50ml/2fl oz/¼ cup double (heavy) cream
1 tablespoon fresh chopped parsley
salt and pepper
225g/8oz puff pastry
beaten egg to glaze

Preheat the oven to 200°C/400°F/gas mark 6. Melt the butter in a pan, add the onions and bay leaf, and cook over a low heat for 5 minutes. Add the garlic and cook for a further 3 minutes. Add the turkey, chestnuts and mushrooms, stirring well to combine everything. Add the flour and cook for 1 minute, stirring continuously. Gradually add the stock, bring to the boil and simmer for 5 minutes. Remove from the heat. Stir in the cream, parsley, salt and pepper. Transfer to a 1.2-litre/2-pint/5-cup pie dish and allow to cool. Roll out the pastry and cover the pie dish. Make a small slit in the centre of the pie, brush with beaten egg and bake for 30–40 minutes.

An elegantly decorated Christmas pie was an important part of the celebratory feast for hundreds of years. Rich fillings of poultry and game were affordable by the wealthy, while the less well-off made do with goose pie. Jack Horner, of nursery rhyme fame, was entrusted with the safe delivery of a Christmas pie to King Henry VIII from his master, the Abbot of Glastonbury. On the journey to London he became curious and looked under the pie crust, where he found not the usual meat and game filling but the title deeds to several Somerset manor houses. He helped himself to the deeds of the Manor of Mells (the 'plum') of the rhyme, which remained in his family for several generations.

The beautifully embellished pie-crust designs were copied by potters of the time. Josiah Wedgwood followed the fashion for these dishes and the buff-coloured examples of Spode pie-crust pottery, although rare, can still be found today.

TRADITIONAL RICH DARK CHRISTMAS PUDDING

This recipe makes 2 large puddings. You can give one as a gift or store it to eat later.

225g/8oz/1¼ cups sultanas (golden raisins)
225g/8oz/1¼ cups raisins
110g/4oz/¾ cup candied peel, chopped
110g/4oz/¾ cup currants
110g/4oz/½ cup ready-to-eat prunes, chopped
150ml/5fl oz/generous ½ cup stout or dark beer
4 tablespoons rum or brandy
175g/6oz/¾ cup shredded suet (shortening)
225g/8oz/4 cups breadcrumbs
225g/8oz/1¼ cups molasses sugar
1 teaspoon grated nutmeg
1 teaspoon ground cinnamon
1 teaspoon ground ginger
pinch of ground cloves
4 eggs, beaten

Place all the fruits in a large mixing bowl with the stout and rum or brandy, cover and leave to soak overnight. Next day, add the rest of the ingredients, stirring well to combine. Divide between 2 × 1.2-litre/2-pint/5-cup greased pudding basins (leaving room for the puddings to rise) and smooth the tops. Cover with a lid or a double thickness of pleated greaseproof (waxed) paper, then with a double thickness of pleated foil. Tie securely and place in 1 or 2 large pans and pour in boiling water to come halfway up the basins. Cover and cook for 6 hours, topping up with boiling water as needed. Cool completely, then wrap in fresh greaseproof paper and foil. Store in a cool, dark place until needed. The puddings will keep for 3 months. To reheat, steam for 2 hours. Serve with rum butter, custard or sweet white sauce.

A TALE OF CHRISTMAS PUDDINGS

Surprisingly, it wasn't until 1865 that special attention was given to Christmas in a cookery book, when *Mrs Beeton's Dictionary of Everyday Cookery* observed 'that it would scarcely be a Christmas dinner without its turkey'. Two recipes for plum pudding were included – a plain one for children and a richer version for adults, with the comment that this was 'seasonable on the 25th December and also at Christmas time'. Mrs Rundell, in her book *A New System of Domestic Cookery* of 1806, stated that 'the plum pudding stands foremost as a truly national dish' but did not associate it with Christmas as it was served all year round.

A rich plum pudding was served to George I on his first Christmas in England in 1714 and this did a great deal to increase its popularity. King George was a great lover of puddings, so much so that he became known as 'the pudding king'. His example was quickly imitated, with everyone who could afford it enjoying a rich plum pudding after their Christmas dinner.

In fact it was in 1836 that plum pudding began to be called 'Christmas pudding' and was first recorded as such in Trollope's *Doctor Thorne*. But it was mainly due to Charles

Dickens that the pudding became the symbol of Christmas cheer, with his description in *A Christmas Carol*: 'the pudding like a speckled cannon-ball, so hard and firm, blazing in half of a quartern of ignited brandy and belight with Christmas holly stuck in the top'.

The origins of the pudding lie in the fifteenth century, when a thick soupy mixture of beef, wine, onions, currants, herbs and spices was thickened with breadcrumbs. Dried plums (prunes) were a Tudor addition and were so popular that 'plums' became a generic term for all dried fruits. By the seventeenth century this mixture had become a special Christmas dish called Christmas or plum porridge, often with the addition of alcohol. By the late eighteenth and early nineteenth centuries the meat was omitted from recipes and the plum pudding that we enjoy today had replaced the porridge.

Charms or coins are traditionally placed in the pudding before cooking and these symbolic items were transferred from the traditional Twelfth Night cake, which was in turn replaced by the Christmas cake.

The Sunday nearest 30 November is the traditional day for making the pudding and is known as 'Stir-up Sunday' because the prayer reading for that day begins, 'Stir up, we beseech Thee, O Lord'. Everyone should have a turn at stirring the mixture from east to west – in honour of the Magi, who travelled in that direction.

SPICED ORANGE RUM BUTTER

A variation of the traditional recipe that's delicious with both Christmas pudding and mince pies.

110g/4oz/1 stick unsalted butter, softened
75g/3oz/3 tablespoons golden caster (milled golden
cane) sugar
50g/2oz/2 tablespoons light muscovado (light brown
muscovado) sugar
4 tablespoons rum
1 teaspoon finely grated orange zest
½ teaspoon ground cinnamon
½ teaspoon ground mixed spice (pumpkin spice)
¼ teaspoon grated nutmeg

Cream the butter until soft and light, then beat in the sugars until soft and fluffy. Gradually beat in the rum a little at a time, then the remaining ingredients. Transfer to a small dish. Cover tightly and chill until needed. This will keep for 1 week in the refrigerator.

RUM BUTTER
TRADITIONS

Why or when sweet, rich rum butter was created is unknown but it has been associated with Cumberland since the eighteenth century. Known as 'brown jam' or 'sweet butter' in local farmhouses, the delicacy was eaten by pregnant women during their confinement and was also given to new mothers to speed their recovery after the ordeal of giving birth. Immediately after birth, the new baby's head was washed with rum and a small piece of rum butter was placed inside its mouth, as its first taste of 'earthly food'. The rum symbolised the spirit of life, butter the goodness of life, sugar the sweetness of life and nutmeg the spice of life.

Large quantities of 'Barbados sugar' and rum were imported from the West Indies, and nutmeg from the Moluccas and the islands of the Dutch East Indies also came into Whitehaven in the eighteenth century. Nutmeg was immensely popular in England at that time and became part of many dishes, along with mace (the lacy outer covering of the nutmeg), cinnamon and cloves. Almost every middle-class household owned a nutmeg grater and most wealthy households possessed silver ones.

In the past, smuggling was rife in the area and local people often took 'damaged' casks home. Legend has it that smugglers would mix the contraband spirit with butter to hide it from excise men! Another story goes that rum butter was created when a cask of rum leaked into an old woman's stores of butter and sugar. The recipe first appeared in print in 1887 in *Mrs A. B. Marshall's Cookery Book*.

Nowadays rum butter is mainly eaten at Christmas with Christmas pudding and mince pies, but it's also delicious with any hot sweet tart or steamed pudding (particularly ginger), and as a filling for sponge sandwich cakes. It will keep for several weeks in the refrigerator.

CLARET JELLY

The gold and silver leaf adds an opulent touch for a special occasion to this alcoholic, grown-up jelly (jello), though if you decide you don't want to use it the jelly still looks splendid on its own.

75g/3oz/3 tablespoons golden caster (milled golden
    cane) sugar
225ml/8fl oz/1 cup water
1 cinnamon stick, broken into pieces
2 cloves
5 leaves gelatine
juice of 1 lemon
300ml/10fl oz/1¼ cups claret
gold and silver leaf to decorate (optional)

Place the sugar, water and spices into a saucepan, cover and bring slowly to the boil. Meanwhile, soak the gelatine leaves for 5 minutes in cold water in a shallow bowl. Remove the pan from the heat and allow to cool slightly. Squeeze the excess moisture from the gelatine leaves and whisk into the warm liquid with the lemon juice. Stir in the lemon juice and claret, then strain into a large jug. Pour into an oiled jelly mould and leave to set. Turn out and decorate with 'stripes' of silver and gold leaf. Alternatively, the jelly can be set in a flat, deep tray and cut into shapes with cookie cutters or cubed before you decorate with the gold and silver leaf.

CHRISTMAS SYLLABUB

A creamy alcoholic concoction with all the flavours of Christmas. Rich but not heavy, this is an elegant and sophisticated alternative to the Christmas pudding.

75g/3oz/½ cup sultanas (golden raisins)
grated zest and juice of 1 large orange
4 tablespoons ginger wine
3 tablespoons dark rum
75g/3oz/½ cup dark muscovado (dark brown
molasses) sugar
600ml/1 pint/2½ cups double (heavy) cream
1 teaspoon ground cinnamon
1 teaspoon ground ginger
50g/2oz/2 tablespoons toasted flaked almonds
chopped crystallised ginger to decorate

Put the sultanas (golden raisins) in a small bowl with the orange zest and pour over the ginger wine and rum. Cover and leave to stand for at least 4 hours. Mix together the orange juice and sugar, stirring until the sugar has dissolved. Strain the liquor from the sultanas into the orange and sugar mixture. Add the cream and spices and beat until thick – be careful not to over-beat. Gently fold in the sultanas and almonds and spoon into serving dishes. Sprinkle with the crystallised ginger. Chill before serving.

GINGER ICE CREAM

An unusual but very good accompaniment to Christmas pudding. Cold and creamy, it makes a great contrast with the hot, steaming pudding.

120ml/4fl oz/½ cup water
75g/3oz/3 tablespoons golden caster (milled golden cane) sugar
3 egg yolks
300ml/10fl oz double (heavy) cream
75g/3oz stem ginger, finely chopped
1 tablespoon stem ginger syrup

Heat the water and sugar in pan over a low heat until the sugar has dissolved. Increase the heat and boil for 2–3 minutes until a little of the cooled syrup will form a thread when drawn between the thumb and forefinger (110°C/225°F on a sugar thermometer). Remove from the heat and cool slightly, then pour on to the egg yolks, whisking all the time until the mixture is thick and mousse-like. Whip the cream until thick but not stiff and fold in the ginger. Carefully fold the ginger cream into the mixture with the ginger syrup. Turn into a freezer-proof container and freeze until firm. Place in the refrigerator 20 minutes before serving.

FRAGRANT
GINGER

The spicy heat of ginger has been enjoyed in Britain for centuries. Available ground, crystallised, candied in syrup or as a fresh root, it is especially delicious as an accompaniment to Christmas pudding. This aromatic spice was known in the late Middle Ages both dried and preserved in syrup. Dried ginger was much cheaper than the preserved type and was sold by the 'race' or hand. Cooks would have peeled and ground the dried root. *The Boke of Nurture* (*c.*1440) recommended preserved ginger as a dessert dish. India and China were both sources of the highly prized ginger and in medieval cookery it was used along with other spices in sauces to accompany meat, poultry and game. Fruit was also often cooked with ginger to enliven the flavour. Ginger remained a favourite spice for hundreds of years. In the early nineteenth century Samuel Taylor Coleridge wrote in a letter to his wife, 'The whole Kingdom is getting Ginger-mad.'

SPARKLING CRYSTALLISED FRUIT CAKE

If you don't like heavy, dark fruit cakes then this light cake made with fruit juices and glacé fruits is the one for you.

175g/6oz/1 cup ready-to-eat dried apricots, chopped
6 tablespoons whisky or brandy
225g/8oz/2 sticks butter
225g/8oz/1¼ cups light muscovado (light brown muscovado) sugar
grated rind and juice of 1 lemon
grated rind and juice of 1 orange
50g/2oz/½ cup ground almonds
4 eggs
225g/8oz/2 cups plain (all-purpose) flour
pinch of salt
175g/6oz/1 cup multicoloured glacé cherries, chopped
110g/4oz/½ cup glacé pineapple, coarsely chopped
110g/4oz/1 cup candied peel, chopped coarsely
50g/2oz/2 tablespoons sultanas (golden raisins)
110g/4oz stem or crystallised ginger, chopped finely
110g/4oz/1 cup walnuts, roughly chopped

for the icing
2 egg whites
450g/1lb/3 cups golden icing (confectioners') sugar
1–2 tablespoons lemon juice
silver and gold balls to decorate

Soak the apricots in the whisky or brandy overnight. Preheat the oven to 150°C/300°F/gas mark
3. Cream the butter and sugar with the lemon and
orange rinds until light and fluffy, then stir in the
almonds. Whisk the eggs until pale and thick, then
gradually whisk into the creamed mixture until
well mixed. Sift the flour and salt into the bowl and
gently fold into the mixture with a metal spoon.
Stir in the orange and lemon juices, soaked
apricots, the candied fruits, sultanas (golden
raisins), ginger and the walnuts. Spoon into a
buttered 23cm/9in round cake tin, lined with a
double thickness of buttered greaseproof (waxed)
paper or non-stick baking parchment and make a
slight hollow in the centre. Bake just below the
centre of the oven for 2½ hours, then cover the cake
loosely with foil and reduce the heat to 140°C/
275°F/gas mark 1 and bake for another 1½–2 hours
until cooked through – test with a skewer, which
should come out clean. Cool the cake in the tin,
then turn out and wrap in greaseproof paper and
foil and store in a cool but not cold place for up to
3 weeks. To make the icing, whisk the egg whites
until frothy and gradually stir in about two-thirds
of the sugar, beating well. Beat in the lemon juice
and the rest of the sugar until the icing is thick and
forms soft peaks. Spoon on to the cold cake and
spread over the cake with a palette knife. Sprinkle
with the silver and gold balls before the icing sets.
Leave to set in a cool but not cold place.

A B R I E F H I S T O R Y O F
C H R I S T M A S C A K E

The modern rich, fruited Christmas cake is the direct descendant of seventeenth-century 'plumb' cakes, which contained 'plumbs' (prunes) and were laced with alcohol. These were in turn descended from the Twelfth Night cake. The snow-white icing was a Victorian invention, as were Christmas cards and decorated Christmas trees.

A lavishly spiced fruit cake was made for the Twelfth Night supper, to celebrate the end of the Christmas festivities. Dating back to the fourteenth century, the cake wasn't iced but was decorated with colourful candied fruits and contained a bean and a pea. The man who found the bean in his slice became king of the festivities for the evening and the woman who found the pea was queen. In later years, charms with symbolic meanings were also hidden in the cake. Pride of place on the table was given to the Twelfth Night pie. When the pie was cut open, a flock of live birds would fly out, to the astonishment and delight of the guests – the source of the reference to 'four and twenty blackbirds baked in a pie' which began to sing when the pie was opened.

Twelfth Night was an immensely popular festive occasion in England, with masques, plays, dancing, singing, gambling and other revelries.

MINCE PIES

225g/8oz shortcrust (pie) pastry
350-450g/12oz–1lb mincemeat
golden icing (confectioners') or golden caster (milled
golden cane) sugar to serve

Preheat the oven to 180°C/ 350°F/gas mark 4.
Roll out the pastry and cut about 14 rounds with
a 9cm/3½in cutter and the same number of
smaller rounds with a 6.5cm/2½in cutter. Line
patty tins with the larger circles and fill with a
teaspoon of mincemeat. Dampen the pastry
edges and cover with the lids. Make a steam hole
in the centre of each and bake for 20–30 minutes
until golden. Cool on a wire rack and dust with
sugar to serve.

CHRISTMAS PIES

The idea of cooking meat with dried fruits and spices originated in the Middle East and was brought back by the Crusaders. A Christmas pie was a popular part of festive fare by Elizabethan times. Shredded meat (mutton or beef) was mixed with suet, cloves, pepper, mace, saffron, raisins, prunes and currants, then the mixture was cooked in a pastry 'coffyn'. The pies were rectangular in shape to represent the manger and were baked without a top, but a pastry 'baby' was put inside to represent the Infant Jesus. These pies were also known as 'shred' or 'minced' pies because of the shredded meat used. Although banned during Cromwell's rule on the grounds that they were idolatrous, Christmas pies made a welcome return with the Restoration, after which they became round instead of rectangular. Over the years, apples and alcohol were added to the ingredients and it was discovered that the mixture could be kept for months in sealed pots as long as the shredded meat was not added until just before cooking.

In time the meat was left out altogether and our modern-day mincemeat was created, the only remnant of the meat content being suet, which is still included.

CUMBERLAND RUM NICKY

75g/3oz/¾ stick butter
110g/4oz/⅔ cup dates, chopped
110g/4oz/¾ cup currants
25g/1oz stem or crystallised ginger, chopped
75g/3oz/½ cup light muscovado (light brown
*   muscovado) sugar*
2 tablespoons dark rum
½ teaspoon freshly grated nutmeg
350g/12oz shortcrust (pie) pastry

Melt the butter and stir in the rest of the ingredients except the pastry. Leave to stand for at least an hour. Preheat the oven to 200°C/400°F/gas mark 6. Roll out the pastry and use half to line a 18cm/7in pie plate. Stir the filling well and spread over the pastry. Cover with the remaining pastry to form a lid and press the edges together firmly to seal. Make a few little cuts across the top. Bake for 30–40 minutes until golden. Serve hot or cold.

This rich and sticky pie is a north of England speciality, incorporating several of the exotic imports which came from Cumberland's trade with the West Indies. Dates, ginger, brown sugar and rum feature in many local dishes. The name is thought to come from the traditional decoration of cuts or 'nicks' on the pastry lid.

OLD ENGLISH EGG NOG TART

This is a rich, creamy custard tart spiced with nutmeg and flavoured with dark rum. It makes a welcome change from the dark, fruity flavours of other Christmas foods.

110g/4oz/1 stick butter
175g/6oz/1¼ cups plain (all-purpose) flour
3 tablespoons ground almonds
6 tablespoons golden caster (milled golden cane) sugar
300ml/10fl oz/1¼ cups milk
¼ teaspoon grated nutmeg
2 eggs, separated
3 teaspoons powdered gelatine
3 tablespoons dark rum
6 tablespoons double (heavy) cream
grated nutmeg to finish

Preheat the oven to 200°C/400°F/gas mark 6. Rub the butter into the flour and stir in the ground almonds and 3 tablespoons sugar. Add a little of the milk and mix to a soft dough. Roll out on a floured board and use to line a deep 20cm/8in flan tin (not loose-based). Bake 'blind' for 10–15 minutes, then leave to cool. Heat the remaining milk with the nutmeg. Beat 2 egg yolks and 1 egg white with the rest of the caster sugar, then pour on the hot (not boiling) milk.

Return the mixture to the pan and heat, stirring, until thick, but do not allow to boil or the mixture will curdle. Remove from the heat and cool slightly. Sprinkle the gelatine over the rum in a small cup and when it 'sponges' (about 5 minutes) stir into the hot custard, stirring well. Leave to stand until beginning to set. Whip the cream until thick but not stiff. Whisk the remaining egg white until stiff. Gently fold the cream into the custard, followed by the egg white. Place the mixture in the baked flan case and chill until set. When set, sprinkle with grated nutmeg and leave at room temperature for 30 minutes before serving.

Egg nog, the traditional Christmas drink in the USA, probably originated in the nineteenth century and is probably a descendant of the medieval caudles – ale mixed with honey and egg yolks – which were believed to be nourishing for those with poor digestion. Here the eggs are cooked along with the traditional ingredients of cream, alcohol and nutmeg to produce a wonderfully rich custard tart.

MARZIPAN SWEETMEATS

Freshly made marzipan is far superior to the commercial variety. This is pale, delicately flavoured and not at all cloyingly sweet. You can tint the marzipan by adding a little food colouring to the almonds and sugar in the mixing bowl.

275g/10oz/1¾ cups ground
almonds
275g/10oz/2 cups golden icing (confectioners')
sugar, sifted, plus extra for kneading
orange flower or rose water
cornflour (cornstarch)

Place the ground almonds and sugar into a mixing bowl and add just enough orange flower or rose water to make a pliable paste. Place the paste in a saucepan and stir over a low heat until it no longer sticks to the sides of the pan. Turn out on to a surface dusted with sugar and cornflour (cornstarch) and knead lightly. Pat or roll out and cut out shapes with festive cutters. Cover lightly and leave in a warm place or a very low oven to dry out. The marzipan should remain pale and soft.

THE ORIGINS OF MARZIPAN

Marzipan, that delectable confection of almonds and sugar, is an essential component of English celebratory cakes, usually concealed under a thick layer of royal icing. At Christmas marzipan sweetmeats shaped realistically into fruits also make their annual appearance.

Marzipan has a fascinating and ancient history. In ancient Persia, the most admired sweet was ground almond paste. Typically it was flavoured with rose water and formed into finger-sized rolls, and was often wrapped in a paper-thin pastry made from egg whites and flour.

When the Arabs conquered Persia (Iran), *lauzinag* as the confection was known, became the favourite dessert in Baghdad. A tenth-century poet compared it to 'a bride's fingers swathed in delicate veils'. *Lauzinag* eventually reached Europe via Spain, where the Moors started calling it by a new name, *makshshabaan*, which was the name of the thin wooden box it was stored in. In Spanish, that word became *mazapan* and in England *marchpane*.

Many legends have grown up about the origin of marzipan, the most famous of which concerns the Lübeck famine of 1407, which is said to have led to the invention of Marcus (St Mark's) bread, or *Marci panis*. When, in 1407, supplies of grain ran out, the Senate is said to have instructed the bakers to make bread using the supplies of almonds stored in the warehouses. However, the same story has appeared in every place where marzipan was made – for example, Venice, Turin and Königsberg – with only the date changing.

In Sicilian and Neapolitan, the words *'martzapane'* and *'marzapane'* were used in the thirteenth century to refer to small boxes, and since spices and confectionery were shipped in these small wooden boxes it may be that the term *'mazaban'* for 'box' may have also referred to the contents.

In the fourteenth century, marzipan developed into artistic creations and figurines modelled by hand. Elizabeth I was very fond of *marchpane* and an elaborately modelled marzipan showpiece, often gilded with gold leaf, was the highlight of grand court feasts.

HIPPOCRAS

1 bottle good red wine
3–4 tablespoons light muscovado (light brown
 muscovado) sugar
2 cinnamon sticks, broken
1 small piece ginger root, bruised
8 cloves
blade of mace
½ teaspoon grated nutmeg
5 cardamom seeds, bruised
strip of orange peel

Put all the ingredients into a pan and slowly bring to simmering point, but do not allow to boil. Simmer very gently for 20 minutes, stirring occasionally. Strain and serve hot.

Hippocras was believed to be a relaxant. On sale ready-made, the ingredients were red or white wine, sweetened with honey or sugar and flavoured with cinnamon, ginger, galingale, cloves, pepper, grains of paradise (a relative of cardamom), cubebs and zedoary (a relative of turmeric, and similar to ginger). The wine was often coloured with turnsole, a purple dye obtained from the plant of the same name, a member of the genus *Heliotropium*. The spices were infused in the wine overnight and strained through the bag before being served with sugar-coated spices such as ginger, candied peels, sugar candy and small ginger 'biscuits' decorated with gold leaf.

LAMBSWOOL

Hot spiced ale, often thickened with eggs or cereal, gradually developed into mulled ales such as Lambswool, which had roasted apples floated on top. The fluffy white apple flesh bursting through the skins was thought to resemble the wool of lambs.

4 eating apples
2.5 litres/4 pints/10 cups ale
6 cloves
1 teaspoon grated nutmeg
½ teaspoon ground ginger
3 whole allspice berries
1 cinnamon stick, broken
½ teaspoon cardamom seeds, bruised
1–2 tablespoons golden caster (milled golden cane)
    sugar

Preheat the oven to 200°C/400°F/gas mark 6. Place the apples in a baking dish with a little ale or water and bake for 30 minutes, until the flesh is 'woolly' in texture. Meanwhile, heat the ale, spices and sugar in a large pan over a low heat until very hot but not boiling. Strain the hot ale into a large bowl or heatproof glasses. Scoop out the apple pulp with a spoon, removing the pips and spread on top of the hot ale.

BASIC RECIPE FOR PANCAKES

110g/4oz/1 cup plain (all-purpose) flour
1 teaspoon golden caster (milled golden cane) sugar
pinch of salt
1 egg
300ml/10fl oz/1¼ cups milk
1 teaspoon oil or melted butter
oil for cooking

Sift the dry ingredients into a mixing bowl and make a well in the centre. Add the egg and beat well. Add half the milk and the oil or butter and beat until smooth. Stir in the rest of the milk. Lightly oil a pancake or frying pan and heat until smoking hot. Add enough batter for a thin, even coating. Cook until set and lightly golden, then turn over and cook for another 30 seconds. Remove from the pan and repeat with the remaining batter, greasing the pan between each pancake.

PANCAKE DAY

Shrove Tuesday (which precedes Ash Wednesday, the start of Lent) is the traditional day for enjoying pancakes throughout England. The custom is very old – the Elizabethans ate pancakes on this day and the term 'pancake' dates back to the fifteenth century.

Along with other animal products, eggs and fat were not allowed during Lent, and as spring is the peak laying time for hens, pancakes were a quick and tasty way to use up surplus eggs. They are probably the only traditional Lenten dish to survive today and it's likely that they developed from the small wheat cakes eaten by pagans in pre-Christian days to celebrate the beginning of spring.

Long ago, the 'shriving bell' was rung from churches throughout England to call people to confess their sins and be shriven (forgiven) – hence the name Shrove Tuesday. The ringing of the bell was also the signal for schoolchildren and people everywhere to leave work for the rest of the day. In Leeds, youths would go round all the schools, beating old tin cans to bring out the scholars to join them, after which they spread further afield until all the schools in the area had been visited and emptied of their pupils! Later still, the church bell was rung at eleven o'clock in the morning as a reminder to housewives to prepare their pancake batter, and so the bell became known as the 'pancake bell'.

Several towns in England have pancake races on Shrove Tuesday, most notably Olney in Buckinghamshire, where the Olney Race is believed to have first been run in 1445. Competitors must be local housewives and they must wear an apron and a hat or scarf. Before the race begins, the pancake bell is rung twice to warn the women to start making their pancakes and then to gather in the town square. Each woman carries a frying pan containing a pancake and the bell rings to start the race. The pancakes must be tossed three times during the race (a distance of 380 metres/415 yards) and the winner and runner-up are awarded a prayer book by the local vicar. The verger can also claim a kiss from the winner! Afterwards, all the frying pans are laid around the font and there is a service of blessing.

QUIRE OF PAPER

These rich but thin and delicate pancakes have the most wonderful elusive flavour, thanks to the orange flower water, sherry and hint of spice.

110g/4oz/1 stick butter
300ml/10fl oz/1¼ cups single (light) cream
75g/3oz/¾ cup plain (all-purpose) flour
1 egg
2 tablespoons medium sherry
1 teaspoon orange flower water
pinch each of grated nutmeg and cinnamon
golden caster (milled golden cane) sugar for
*   sprinkling*

Melt the butter and remove from the heat. Add to the other ingredients and beat well to a batter. Grease a 15cm/6in frying or omelette pan with butter and pour in just enough batter to coat the base thinly. As soon as the mixture sets, turn carefully with a palette knife – the edges will be very delicate. Pile on to a warm plate, sprinkling sugar between each pancake. You shouldn't need to grease the pan every time as the mixture is very rich. It should be enough to make 10 thin pancakes.

> So named because they are paper-thin, these elegant cream pancakes were a great favourite in the early eighteenth century.

HOT CROSS BUNS

Homemade hot cross buns are so much nicer than shop-bought ones. The kitchen fills with the glorious scents of fruits and spices as the buns cook. Eat them warm and straight from the oven to appreciate them at their best.

450g/1lb/4 cups strong white bread flour
1 teaspoon salt
1 teaspoon ground cinnamon
1 teaspoon ground mixed spice (pumpkin spice)
¼ teaspoon grated nutmeg
50g/2oz/½ stick butter
50g/2oz/¼ cup golden granulated (milled golden cane) sugar
25g/1oz fresh yeast
175ml/6fl oz/¾ cup warm milk
1 egg, beaten
110g/4oz/¾ cup currants
50g/2oz/½ cup candied peel, chopped

for the glaze
2 tablespoons milk
2 tablespoons water
2 tablespoons golden caster (milled golden cane) sugar

Sift the flour, salt and spices into a large mixing bowl. Rub in the butter until the mixture resembles breadcrumbs. Reserve 1 teaspoon

sugar and stir the rest into the flour. Cream the
yeast with the reserved sugar until liquid, then
stir into the milk and leave until frothy. Pour into
the flour with the egg and mix well to a soft
dough. Turn out on to a floured surface and
knead until smooth and elastic. Place in an oiled
bowl, cover and leave in a warm place for 1 hour
to rise. Preheat the oven to 200°C/400°F/gas
mark 6. Work the currants and peel into the
dough, kneading well. Divide into 12 pieces and
shape into buns. Place on greased baking sheets,
cover and leave in a warm place to prove for 25
minutes. Cut a cross in the top of each bun with a
sharp knife, then bake for 20 minutes until
golden. Meanwhile, heat the ingredients for the
glaze in a small pan. Simmer for 2 minutes, then
2 minutes before the end of the cooking time
brush the buns with glaze and return to the oven.
Remove from the oven and brush with more
glaze while hot. Cool on a wire rack.

A BRIEF HISTORY OF HOT CROSS BUNS

Hot cross buns are traditionally eaten on Good Friday morning for breakfast. In the past, street sellers would be out before dawn, hawking their freshly baked hot buns. These early hot cross buns were richer than today's versions, containing saffron as well as other less costly spices. A bun would often be saved until the following year for good luck and, according to legend, it might become hard but would never go mouldy. In years gone by, hot cross buns were baked only on Good Friday – in 1792, for example, those from the Chelsea Bun House (see page 211) were reputed to be particularly good. All bread dough was once marked with a cross to ward off any evil influences that might prevent it from rising during baking, but this practice was banned by the Puritans on the grounds that it was Papist. However, they did allow bread baked on Good Friday to retain its cross in order to commemorate the Crucifixion.

Fruited breads were very popular in Tudor England and were originally for festive occasions. In 1592 bakers were forbidden to make them except for funerals, Good Friday and Christmas. If they flouted this law, any buns or bread had to be given free to the poor. The law was still in effect in 1784 and may have been the origin of the custom of distributing hot cross buns to the poor of the parish. By the time of James I, it had become difficult to enforce and died out.

TRADITIONAL SIMNEL CAKE

A rich fruit cake that's best made a few weeks before you need it to allow the flavours to develop gradually.

110g/4oz/1 stick butter
100g/4oz/¾ cup light muscovado (light brown muscovado) sugar
3 eggs, beaten
150g/5oz/1¼ cups plain (all-purpose) flour
1 teaspoon baking powder
¼ teaspoon salt
1 teaspoon ground mixed spice (pumpkin spice)
½ teaspoon freshly grated nutmeg
½ teaspoon ground cinnamon
350g/12oz/2 cups mixed raisins, currants and sultanas (golden raisins)
50g/2oz/½ cup candied peel, chopped
finely grated zest of 1 lemon
450g/1lb marzipan
a little apricot jam for glazing
beaten egg to glaze

Preheat the oven to 170°C/325°F/gas mark 3. Cream the butter and sugar together until fluffy. Gradually beat in the eggs a little at a time. Sift the flour, baking powder, salt and spices together and add to the mixture alternately with the mixed fruit, peel and lemon zest. Mix well. Put half the mixture into a greased, lined 18cm/7in loose-bottomed, round cake tin and smooth the top. Roll out most of the marzipan (reserve some for eleven balls for decoration) into two rounds large enough to fit the cake tin. Place one round on top of the cake mixture and press lightly. Cover with the rest of the cake mixture and smooth the top, hollowing the centre slightly. Bake for 1½–2 hours, then cool in the tin. When the cake is cold, brush the top with warmed apricot jam. Lay the remaining circle of marzipan on top of the cake. Form 11 small balls from the reserved marzipan and place them around the edge in a circle. Brush the marzipan with beaten egg and put the cake into the oven for about 5 minutes at 200°C/450°F/gas mark 6 until the marzipan is lightly browned.

THE STORY OF
SIMNEL CAKES

Simnel cakes (the name may come from the Latin *simnellus*, meaning fine flour, or from the Anglo-Saxon word for a feast, *symel*) were taken home by servant girls on Mothering Sunday, the fourth Sunday in Lent, which was one of the few days they were allowed home to visit their families. Early versions were thin, crisp wafers made from fine flour and stamped with a likeness of Jesus or Mary. As time passed, simnel cakes evolved into fruited bread and by the end of the seventeenth century had become a rich fruit cake with a layer of marzipan in the middle. Simnel cakes were so popular on Mothering Sunday that it became known as Simnel Sunday. The poet Robert Herrick (1591–1674) mentioned the cakes in one of his poems:

> *I'll to thee a Simnell bring*
> *'Gainst thou goest a mothering.*
> *So that, when she blesseth thee,*
> *Half that blessing thou'lt give me.*

The cake gradually acquired a marzipan topping and later became associated with Easter. Simnel cakes were usually decorated with eleven or twelve almond paste balls to represent the Apostles. Many people omitted Judas, but others preferred to include the full complement. One tradition was to engrave a figure of Jesus in the centre of the cake with the almond paste balls surrounding the image. The top can be browned under a grill rather than in a hot oven.

Today, simnel cakes are also decorated with crystallised spring flowers, fluffy chicks and coloured eggs made from sugar or chocolate.

Rich fruity tea breads originated as a sideline to bread making and were made by adding dried fruits, sugar, butter and spices to plain bread dough. Due to the high cost of the imported ingredients these enriched breads were served only on special occasions.

In the bakehouses and kitchens of the wealthy, tea breads gave way to enormous fruitcakes baked in large ovens, which were served on important occasions. Before the invention of cake tins, early cakes were shaped by hand into rounds and put into a tin hoop (which helped to keep the cake in shape) placed on a tin tray before baking.

EASTER CHOCOLATE NEST CAKE

This gluten- and wheat-free lusciously rich, dense chocolate cake resembles a soufflé with its mousse-like texture. It will sink in the centre as it cools to form the 'nest', which can then be filled with whipped cream, fromage frais, crystallised violet petals, mini-eggs, and so on. It's best eaten on the day of making.

225g/8oz plain (semi-sweet) chocolate (minimum
    60% cocoa solids)
50g/2oz/½ stick butter
2 tablespoons rum or orange juice
6 eggs, separated
75g/3oz/½ cup light muscovado (light brown
    muscovado) sugar

Preheat the oven to 160°C/325°F/gas mark 3. Break the chocolate into pieces and place in a heatproof bowl with the butter. Place the bowl over a pan of simmering water (the water must not boil or the chocolate will become thick and lumpy) until the chocolate has melted. Stir in the rum or orange juice. Whisk the egg yolks in a large bowl with 50g/2oz/2 tablespoons sugar until thick. Stir in the chocolate mixture. In a separate bowl whisk the egg whites until softly peaking and gradually whisk in the rest of the sugar to form a stiff, shiny meringue. Gently fold a third of the meringue into the chocolate mixture, then fold in the remainder until thoroughly combined. Turn into a greased, lined 23cm/9in spring-form cake tin and bake for 35 minutes until well risen and beginning to crack on the surface. Leave to cool in the tin for 15 minutes, then carefully remove the sides of the tin and leave to become cold on a wire rack. Transfer to a serving plate and fill the centre with your chosen filling.

J S Fry (now part of the Cadbury empire) created the first chocolate Easter eggs in 1873. These were made of dark chocolate and were filled with sweets. Cadbury's launched the first Dairy Milk chocolate egg in 1905. Easter eggs account for 8 per cent of all chocolate sales today, with Cadbury's Creme Eggs easily the most popular choice – over 300 million are made each year. If these were stacked on top of each other, they would be ten times higher than Mount Everest!

HINDLE WAKES

1 large (2.2kg/5lb) chicken
150ml/5fl oz/generous ½ cup red wine vinegar
few sprigs fresh parsley
1 bay leaf
25g/1oz/1 tablespoon light muscovado (light brown
muscovado) sugar

for the stuffing
450g/1lb/2 cups ready-to-eat prunes, roughly
chopped
110g/4oz/2 cups fresh breadcrumbs
110g/4oz/½ cup blanched almonds, roughly chopped
2 tablespoons finely chopped fresh mixed herbs
salt and pepper
50g/2oz/¼ cup shredded suet (shortening)
150ml/5fl oz/generous ½ cup red wine

for the sauce
600ml/1 pint/2½ cups chicken stock (see recipe)
1½ tablespoons butter
1½ tablespoons flour
grated zest of 1 lemon
150ml/5fl oz/generous ½ cup double (heavy) cream
lemon slices and prunes to garnish

Mix the stuffing ingredients together and pack into the chicken, securing the vent so that no stuffing can escape. Put the chicken into a large pan with enough water to almost cover it and add the wine vinegar, parsley, bay leaf and sugar to the pan. Bring to the boil, cover and simmer for about 3 hours until the chicken is cooked. Remove the chicken from the pan and place on a serving plate. Skim the fat from the stock and measure out the 600ml/1 pint/2½ cups for the sauce. Melt the butter in a pan and stir in the flour. Gradually add the chicken stock and cook gently for 10 minutes, stirring constantly until thickened. Add the lemon zest and season to taste. Leave to cool. Whip the cream until thickened and fold into the cooled sauce. Pour over the chicken to coat completely and garnish.

Hindle Wakes was a medieval Lancashire dish, although an old hen would have been used instead of a chicken. The night before the dish was to be eaten, a boiling fowl was stuffed with a mixture of prunes, nuts and spices and simmered slowly until tender. The next morning the bird was removed from the stock, coated with a lemon sauce, then decorated with prunes and slices of lemon. It was always served cold. The strong contrast of the white chicken meat, black stuffing and black and yellow garnish made for a strikingly colourful main dish. The curious name may derive from 'Hen de la Wake' – in Lancashire dialect a wake was a fair. The recipe is thought to have been brought by Flemish weavers to Bolton-le-Moor, near Wigan, in 1337.

SALMON IN WHITE WINE

Cold poached salmon with new potatoes is one of the glories of an English summer. You don't need a fish kettle – a roasting tin or ovenproof dish will be fine.

approx. 2.5kg/3lb whole salmon, gutted and cleaned
approx. 350ml/12fl oz/1½ cups fish stock
approx. 350ml/12fl oz/1½ cups dry white wine
few peppercorns
slices of lemon
bay leaf
parsley and lemon wedges to garnish

Preheat the oven to 170°C/325°F/gas mark 3. Place the fish in a large roasting tin or ovenproof dish, curving it to fit. Mix the fish stock and wine and pour over the fish. The liquid should come halfway up the fish. Add the remaining ingredients and cover with buttered foil – don't let the foil touch the fish. Cook for about 1–1¼ hours, basting from time to time, until cooked through. Test the middle part of the salmon to check. Cover and leave to cool in the liquid. When the fish is cold, lift it very carefully on to a work surface and peel off the skin and discard. Turn over and repeat on the other side. Lift carefully on to a large serving plate. You can decorate the fish with wafer-thin slices of

cucumber, if liked, to represent scales. Garnish
with fresh parsley and lemon wedges.

Peppercorns were the most popular spice introduced to
England by the Romans. In the Middle Ages the spice
trade was organised by the Guild of Pepperers, one of
the oldest of the London guilds (they were called
grocers from 1370). Some medieval landlords fixed
rents in weights of pepper, hence the term 'peppercorn
rent'. Whole peppercorns retain their warm, aromatic
flavour better than ground pepper.

SUMMER BERRY CUSTARD TART

Ripe, luscious summer berries are a joy. Here
they are married with a rich, thick custard in a
crisp pastry case. You can buy the case ready-
made to save time.

75g/3oz/¾ stick butter
50g/2oz/¼ cup golden caster (milled
golden cane) sugar
1 tablespoon cornflour (cornstarch)
4 egg yolks, beaten
1 teaspoon vanilla essence (extract)
600ml/1 pint/2½ cups double (heavy) or
whipping cream
25cm/10in baked pastry case
350g/12oz/2 cups fresh raspberries
225g/8oz/1¼ cups strawberries
2 tablespoons golden icing (confectioners') sugar,
sifted

Heat the butter, sugar and cornflour (cornstarch)
in a heavy pan over a medium heat, stirring
constantly until the mixture thickens and boils.
Boil for 1 minute and remove from the heat. Stir a
small amount into the beaten egg yolks, then
slowly pour into the remaining mixture in the
pan, stirring all the time to prevent lumps
forming. Cook, stirring all the time, until the
mixture thickens enough to coat the back of the

spoon – about 1 minute. Remove from the heat, add the vanilla and leave to cool. Cover and chill until very cold. Whip half the cream until thick but not stiff and fold into the cold custard. Spoon the custard evenly into the pastry case. Arrange the raspberries in circles around the edge of the tart and fill the centre with strawberries. Chill for 1 hour until the custard has set. Whisk the remaining cream with the golden icing (confectioners') sugar until thick and spoon into a piping bag. Pipe rosettes on to the chilled tart.

Wild raspberries were known in medieval England as raspes or hindberries. The reason for the latter is that the berries were eaten by deer, but it's not known why they were named raspes. The sweet berries were first cultivated as a garden fruit in the sixteenth century and by the seventeenth they were known as raspberries.

VICTORIAN-STYLE ICED PUDDING

A sumptuous dessert that's not difficult to make.

50g/2oz/¼ cup sultanas (golden
raisins)
50g/2oz/¼ cup glacé cherries
50g/2oz/½ cup crystallised pineapple
1 wine glass brandy
6 egg yolks
finely grated zest of 1 orange
finely grated zest of 1 lemon
900ml/1½ pints/4 cups creamy milk
50g/2oz/¼ cup golden caster (milled
golden cane) sugar
25g/1oz powdered gelatine
600ml/1 pint/2½ cups double (heavy) cream
2 teaspoons orange liqueur

Soak the fruits in the brandy in a small bowl for at least 2 hours. Whisk the egg yolks with the orange and lemon zests, milk and sugar in a heatproof bowl. Sprinkle the gelatine over a little cold water in a small bowl and leave to stand for 5 minutes. When dissolved, beat into the egg mixture. Place the bowl over a pan of hot (not boiling) water and beat until the mixture thickens. Stir in half the cream, all the liqueur and the brandy-soaked fruits. Let the mixture thicken again over the hot water, stirring all the time, but don't allow it to boil or it will curdle. Pour into a 1.5-litre/2½-pint/6¼-cup container or mould and chill in the refrigerator until cold, then freeze for at least 4 hours. About 20 minutes before serving, whip the remaining cream until thick. Turn out the pudding and cover with the cream.

An elaborately moulded ice confection was the high point of affluent Victorian dinners and buffets. The moulds were made of pewter and were designed in the shape of fruits, flowers, fish and even vegetables. These are now highly prized collectors items.

Mrs Agnes Marshall was the queen of ice cream. She started a cookery school in 1857, lectured and wrote articles. Her 'Book of Ices' (1870) contained basic recipes and was followed in 1894 by another book 'Fancy Ices' with more complicated recipes for moulded iced desserts.

QUICK ICED PUDDING

At least one elaborately moulded iced pudding was served at a formal Victorian dinner or banquet. Frozen confections were described as 'iced puddings' and were very fashionable during the 1920s and 1930s, when more households acquired refrigerators.

450g/1lb Madeira cake
300ml/10fl oz/1¼ cups double (heavy) cream
1 tablespoon golden icing (confectioners') sugar
5 tablespoons ginger wine or rum
2 pieces stem or crystallised ginger, finely chopped
110g/4oz/½ cup candied fruits, quartered

Split the cake lengthways into 3 slices. Line a 450g/1lb loaf tin with cling film (plastic wrap). Whip the cream and sugar with 2 tablespoons ginger wine or rum to stiff peaks. Fold in the stem ginger. Place 1 slice of cake in the base of the loaf tin and sprinkle with a third of the remaining wine or rum. Cover with half the cream and half the remaining wine or rum. Top with a slice of cake. Cover with the rest of the cream and the candied fruits. Top with the remaining cake and sprinkle with the rest of the wine or rum. Cover with foil and freeze for at least 4 hours. Turn out just before serving and cut into slices.

PARKIN

The flavour and texture of parkin are greatly improved if it's stored, wrapped, in an airtight tin for at least 3 days before eating.

175g/6oz/1½ cups plain (all-purpose) flour
1 teaspoon salt
2 teaspoons ground ginger
1 teaspoon ground cinnamon
1 teaspoon grated nutmeg
1 teaspoon bicarbonate of soda
*   (baking soda)*
275g/10 oz/1¼ cups medium oatmeal (uncooked)
175g/6oz/generous ½ cup black treacle (molasses)
150g/5oz/1¼ sticks butter
110g/4oz/¾ cup dark muscovado (dark brown
*   molasses) sugar*
150ml/5fl oz/generous ½ cup milk
1 egg

Preheat the oven to 180°C/350°F/gas mark 4. Sift together the flour, salt, spices and bicarbonate of soda (baking soda) and stir in the oatmeal. In a saucepan, melt the treacle (molasses), butter, sugar and milk together, then cool to lukewarm. Beat in the egg. Pour the liquid mixture into the dry ingredients and beat well until smooth. Pour into a greased, lined 18cm/7in square tin and bake for 1 hour. Cool in the tin for 5 minutes, then turn out and cool on a wire rack.

YORKSHIRE PARKIN

There's an old Yorkshire saying addressed to anyone who's feeling under the weather, 'Don't worry. You'll soon be like a parkin.' Traditionally eaten in the county on Bonfire Night, 5 November (in Leeds in the nineteenth century, 5 November was called Parkin Day), parkin is a dark, spicy, solid gingerbread made with oatmeal, flour, spices and black treacle. In Yorkshire it's often enjoyed with a piece of cheese. The term parkin was first recorded in the nineteenth century, but its origins are unknown. In Scotland there's a similarly named type of ginger biscuit called a perkin.

In the northern counties of Lancashire and Yorkshire, Bonfire Night celebrations would be unthinkable without parkin. Originally it was a celebratory cake, eaten at winter festivals, a custom which probably originated with the pagan practice of eating special cakes to celebrate the first day of winter. In parts of Lancashire, parkin was known as harcake or soul cake, and was traditionally associated with All Souls' Day (2 November). It was cooked on a bakestone by the hearth and was also known as tharve (hearth) cake. Housewives in Lancashire and Yorkshire pride themselves on their home baking, particularly the making of these types of hearty, satisfying cake. The parkins in days gone by were plainer and dryer than the type we know today. Poorer families would have used dripping instead of butter and the original recipe did not use eggs. Oats were the main cereal grown in the north, and are responsible for the solid texture of the cake. Ginger was by far the cheapest spice available, although it was still a treat for most ordinary people.

In the seventeenth century treacle was introduced into England and quickly became a cheap and popular substitute for honey. Imported from the West Indies, it was obtained easily by those who lived near the ports of Lancashire and was incorporated into the recipe.

By the eighteenth century, as basic ingredients such as flour and sugar became cheaper and more widely available, they too were included, resulting in a lighter cake. Yorkshire parkin recipes generally use more oatmeal than flour, while Lancashire recipes tend to have more flour than oatmeal. There are many different kinds of parkin (every family has its own favourite recipe) and it continues to be popular in the north, where it is on sale in bakers throughout the region ready for 5 November.

BEEF WELLINGTON

Fillet is one of the tastiest and most tender cuts of beef. Quite expensive, it is perfect for a special occasion. Adding pâté or, even more luxurious, foie gras and/or duxelles, a mixture of minced mushrooms and onions, then wrapping the fillet in crisp pastry will stretch it to serve 4 people generously.

450g/1lb fillet of beef in one piece
salt and pepper
50g/2oz/½ stick butter
1 tablespoon oil
1 small onion, finely chopped
175g/6oz mushrooms, finely chopped
2 tablespoons brandy
2 tablespoons freshly chopped parsley
350g/12oz puff pastry
110g/4oz liver pâté
beaten egg to glaze

Preheat the oven to 230°C/450°F/gas mark 8. Trim the fat from the meat and sprinkle with salt and pepper. Heat the butter and oil in a frying pan and, when hot, add the meat and brown it evenly on all sides. Remove from the pan and allow the meat to cool. Add the onion and mushrooms to the pan and cook gently until soft but not browned. Stir in the brandy and parsley, and continue cooking until the liquid has evaporated. Season with salt and pepper and leave until cold. Roll out the pastry in a rectangle large enough to enclose the meat. Beat the pâté until smooth and spread over the top and sides of the meat. Brush the pastry with a little of the beaten egg. Spoon half the mushroom mixture over the pastry and place the beef fillet, pâté side down, on top. Spread the remaining pâté on the top of the beef, then spread with the rest of the mushroom mixture. Brush one long side of pastry with beaten egg. Fold the unbrushed side over the beef, then fold the second side over and press together to seal. Join the ends of the pastry in a pinched frill and trim off any excess. Use the trimmings to make leaves to decorate the pastry. Cut 2 slits in the top of the pastry to allow the steam to escape and brush the top with the remaining beaten egg. Place on a baking tray and bake for 10 minutes, then reduce the heat to 180°C/350°F/gas mark 4 and continue cooking for another 20–30 minutes until the pastry is golden. Rest for 10 minutes before cutting into thick slices to serve.

This tasty recipe for steak wrapped in puff pastry is named after Arthur Wellesley, the 1st Duke of Wellington, who became a national hero after defeating Napoleon at the Battle of Waterloo in 1815.

CINNAMON-SCENTED RICE PUDDING BRÛLÉE

We all have our favourite rice pudding – thick and creamy, soft and milky, with or without a golden-brown skin. Luckily, everyone who has tried this elegantly rich version of the dessert, with its crisp toffee topping, has enjoyed it.

75g/3oz pudding rice
850ml/1½ pints/4 cups rich, creamy milk
1 cinnamon stick
110g/4oz/½ cup golden caster (milled golden cane)
    sugar, plus 4–6 tablespoons
2½ leaves gelatine
150ml/5fl oz/generous ½ cup double (heavy) cream
few drops vanilla essence (extract)

Put the rice into a pan with the milk, cinnamon stick and 110g/4oz/½ cup sugar, and bring to the boil, stirring. Cover and cook very gently until the rice is tender and has absorbed most of the milk – about 30–40 minutes. Remove the cinnamon stick. Then soak the gelatine leaves in a bowl of cold water for 5 minutes. Squeeze to remove the excess moisture. Whisk the cream and

gelatine together. Stir into the warm rice mixture with the vanilla essence (extract). Pour into 4 lightly buttered ramekin dishes and leave to cool. Chill until ready to add the brûlée topping. Sprinkle the puddings evenly with the remaining sugar and place under a very hot grill until the sugar is bubbling. Leave to cool, but don't put them in the refrigerator.

In the seventeenth and eighteenth centuries rice puddings were rather more grand affairs than the nursery fare of later years. Baked rice pudding was flavoured with rose water or wine, spices such as ginger, nutmeg and mace, and was enriched with eggs and fat.

Porters English Restaurant
17 Henrietta Street
Covent Garden
London WC2E 8QH
Tel: 020 7836 6466

For online bookings, up-to-date menus and very special offers visit:
www.porters-restaurant.com

Porters English Restaurant, now celebrating its 25th anniversary, is still owned by Lord Bradford. It specialises in home-made English food, with bestsellers including Steak, Guinness and Mushroom Pie, Wild Boar and Sage Sausages, and Traditional Roast Beef, not to mention wonderful puddings like Steamed Syrup Sponge, Spotted Dick, and Apple and Blackberry Crumble. Starters and puddings are £3.60, while most main courses are just £8.95. Porters also prides itself on its transparent pricing policy: for instance, there is no cover charge, bread is included with all starters and an appropriate side order is included with every main course. But don't just take our word for it . . .

'In 1979 the 7th Earl of Bradford opened this restaurant, stating, "It will serve real English food at affordable prices", and he has succeeded notably – and not just because Lady Bradford turned over her carefully guarded recipe for banana and ginger steamed pudding. A comfortable, two-storied restaurant with a friendly, informal and lively atmosphere, Porters specializes in classic English pies, including Old English fish pie; lamb and apricot; ham, leek and cheese; and of course, bangers and mash' – *Frommer's*

'Good British food (really), an Olde Worlde public house interior, a nob owner (the Earl of Bradford), and a reasonable check – no wonder Americans invariably like this place. Pies star on the menu – lamb and apricot or chicken and chilli alongside the traditional fish or steak and kidney, with steamed sponges and custard for afters' – *Fodor's*

'One is tempted to say that before dining at Porters one should check with Mother and double-check with Nanny that it is all right to have such an unashamed indulgence. Prepare to return to the good old days and the reassurance that wholesome English food is what made the Empire great and can still delight and embolden the visitor to Covent Garden' – *Covent Garden Life*

And finally . . . some things that you might not have known about Porters English Restaurant. During the past 25 years Porters has served over three million people, who have consumed:

- more onions than Wimbledon has used tennis balls in 25 championships;
- enough lettuce to fill all 32 pods of the London Eye;
- so many beef faggots that, if stacked, they would be 20 times higher than Canary Wharf;
- the equivalent weight in chicken to 62 Mini Coopers;
- enough sausages to draw a line from Covent Garden to Oxford!

ACKNOWLEDGEMENTS

My thanks to the following for their invaluable help – it has been a real pleasure to work with every one of them.

Richard, Earl of Bradford, who came up with the idea of the book and generously shared Porters recipes and who, like me, believes that English food is among the best in the world.

My husband Gordon and son Ivan for their support and helpful advice as they tested many of the recipes.

Billingtons, who supplied the unrefined sugars used in the recipes.

Lesley Levene and Miranda Stonor, who painstakingly edited the book.

And last, but by no means least, Jeremy Robson and Jane Donovan at Robson Books for their helpful encouragement and guidance.

Carol Wilson

I heartily echo Carol's acknowledgements to everyone involved in the book. I would also like to thank Joanne, my wife, who cooks marvellous English food – her Yorkshire puddings are appreciated even by Yorkshiremen. And to the staff at Porters elsewhere.

Richard, Earl of Bradford

INDEX